SUBCULTURE TO CLUBCULTURES

An Introduction to Popular Cultural Studies

Steve Redhead

Photographs by Patrick Henry

BLACKWELL
Publishers

The right of Steve Redhead to be identified as author of this work has been asserted in accordance with the Copyright, Designs and Patents Act 1988.

First published 1997

First published in USA

2 4 6 8 10 9 7 5 3 1

Blackwell Publishers Ltd
108 Cowley Road
Oxford OX4 1JF
UK

Blackwell Publishers Inc.
350 Main Street
Malden, Massachusetts 02148
USA

British Library Cataloguing in Publication Data

A CIP catalogue record for this book is available from the British Library.

Library of Congress-Cataloging-in-Publication Data

Redhead, Steve, 1952–
    Subculture to clubcultures : an introduction to popular cultural
studies / Steve Redhead.
        p.   cm.
    Includes bibliographical references and index.
        ISBN 0–631–19788–5 (acid-free paper). — ISBN 0–631–19789–3 (pbk.
    : acid-free paper)
    1. Subculture–Great Britain.   2. Youth–Great Britain–Social
life and customs.   3. Popular culture—Great Britain.   4. Popular
music—Great Britain.   5. Music and youth—Great Britain.
I. Title.
HN383.5.R43 1997
305.235'0941—dc21   96-39887
                                                                                    CIP

Typeset in 10½ on 12pt Bembo
by Grahame & Grahame Editorial, Brighton

Printed and bound in Great Britain by
Marston Lindsay Ross International Ltd,
Oxfordshire

Contents

Acknowledgements

Acknowledgement is due to Buddy Holly, Nick Lowe, I Ludicrous, the Smiths and Oasis for the song titles which I have borrowed or bastardized in the titles for some of the chapters in this book.

I would like to thank the various editors who have published my work in this field over the years. Some parts of this book have appeared in very different versions in journals such as *Labour Leader, New Statesman, New Statesman and Society, Marxism Today, New Socialist, New Society, Sociological Review* and *City Life*. Thanks to all those who helped to ensure that the published versions saw the light of day at the time. I am also grateful to all of the researchers who have worked jointly with me at the Manchester Metropolitan University (formerly Manchester Polytechnic) during the 'Thatcher and Major years' and the publishers of my books on the regulation of youth culture in these 'hard times': namely, *Sing When You're Winning* (Pluto Press, London), *The End-of-the-Century Party* (Manchester University Press, Manchester) and *Football with Attitude, Rave Off: politics and deviance in contemporary youth culture* and *The Passion and the Fashion: football fandom in the new Europe* (Ashgate Publishing, Aldershot). Various academic colleagues in the United Kingdom have written collaborative pieces with me since the watershed election in 1979: Eugene McLaughlin, Antonio Melechi and Andy Lovatt respectively worked with me on the research which is written up here under 'Thatcher's Boys (Next Door)', 'Pop Time, Acid House', 'Supertifo' and 'Licensed to Thrill'. Thanks to all of them for their stimulating and insightful participation. Thanks, too, to Patrick Henry, whose excellent photographs have adorned several of my books so appropriately. Last but not least, many thanks to Helen Walker and all her colleagues in the School of Law general office at the Manchester Metropolitan University.

Introduction

What I have elsewhere labelled 'Popular Cultural Studies' consists of a critical homage to cultural theory of the past – through pastiche, parody, plunder, irony – just as popular music culture replays and reworks its own past in order to invent and create a new modern art form.[1] 'Pop Cult Studs[2] might be a more apt label to distinguish it from Cultural Studies and high theory *per se*.

Just as earlier work came out of the particular research conditions of the Centre for Contemporary Cultural Studies at the University of Birmingham in the 1970s, this book stems from research in the department – and eventually the School – of Law at Manchester Polytechnic, which became the Manchester Metropolitan University in 1992. Many people have been associated with this work since the late 1970s, especially the various ethnographers at the Unit for Law and Popular Culture set up in the School of Law in 1990, and which from 1992 until 1995 was part of the Manchester Institute for Popular Culture at the Manchester Metropolitan University. Original ethnographic and oral history research into popular music and youth culture – especially the long trajectory which mixed soccer hooligans and crusties with pop kids and spawned rave culture[3] – is the backcloth to the book and has already produced edited books of original cultural studies and criminology essays in Ashgate's Popular Cultural Studies series, as well as my introduction to the field in *The End-of-the-Century Party: youth and pop towards 2000*, published by Manchester University Press (in Manchester and New York) in 1990.

What I proclaimed as 'Popular Cultural Studies' in *Unpopular Cultures*, also published by Manchester University Press, builds on the rich legacy of Contemporary Cultural Studies – and especially the 'Birmingham

School' – but also repairs some of the theoretical, political and method-
ological problems generated by that previous body of work. Specifically,
the notion of 'subculture' (Dick Hebdige's chosen title and the label taken
for much of the categorization of the Birmingham School's work on youth
and popular music) is seen to be no longer appropriate – if, indeed, it ever
was – to conceptual apparatuses needed to explain pop music culture's
developments since the publication of Hebdige's major book in 1979. The
late 1970s and early 1980s marked the start of an extended free-market
experiment in New Right government in the UK, the USA and many
other countries, which forms the political, economic and cultural conditions for the moment of what some writers have called 'club cultures'
(Thornton, 1995). If the moment of 'subculture' was the punk spirit of
1976, the moment of clubcultures was probably 1988 – the second
'summer of love'.

'Clubcultures' is the concept, and global youth formation, which supple-
ments 'subculture' as the key to the analysis of the histories and futures of
youth culture. This book forms a long commentary on *Subculture* (Hebdige, 1979). It breaks new political ground, but retains the Centre for
Contemporary Cultural Studies' emphasis on mixing original ethnography
with exciting and innovative social theory and political commentary. The
book takes its inspiration from varieties of contemporary popular music:
from post-punk to indie through soccer terrace 'folk' songs to house/post-
house[4] dance music from the late 1970s onwards, and the reader should be
able to hear its echoes on the printed page. The history it presents dates from
the post-punk era of the late 1970s through the hidden origins of the summer
of love back in the late 1980s to the internationalization – or globalization-
of sport- and music-influenced youth and dance club culture in the 1990s,
involving a waning – in the UK at least – of 'rock-ist' culture and the rise
of the DJ/producer. The history is based on first-hand research and unique
archive collections of music, videos, fanzines, flyers, memorabilia and
personal interviews.

So at the *fin de millennium*, 'The beat goes on' into the twenty-first century.
Thirty years on from the Situationists' warning shots, we are now, finally,
leaving the twentieth century. If, as I argued in *The End-of-the-Century Party*,
'pop time' had accelerated by 1989 to such an extent that we were in danger
of missing out the last decade altogether, the conditions for 'youth and pop'
after 2000 are likely to contain as much a feeling of *déjà vu* as for the past
twenty years.

In 1994 the Criminal Justice and Public Order Act received Royal Assent
in the British Parliament. Section 63 ('Powers to Remove Persons Attending
or Preparing for a Rave') attempted to enshrine in law for the first time a
criminalization of certain forms of music. Section 63(1)(b) defined the music
as 'sounds wholly or predominantly characterised by the emission of a

succession of repetitive beats'. In the late 1980s an earlier bill, passed as the Entertainments (Increased Penalties) Act 1990, introduced new maximum penalties (a fine of £20,000, six months' imprisonment or both) for breaches of already existing legislation, affecting both public and private entertainment, licensing places which 'are used for music, dancing or similar'. Such legal amendment to the Local Government Act 1963, the Private Places of Entertainment Act 1967, the Local Government (Miscellaneous Provisions) Act 1982 and the Civic Government (Scotland) Act 1982 was supposedly aimed at the 'acid house' phase of contemporary dance music culture. Acid house as a term was already long out of fashion by the time the bill became an Act of Parliament in 1990. 'Rave' would probably have been more appropriate as a descriptive label. By 1994, when the Criminal Justice and Public Order Act passed into law, 'rave', too, was past its sell-by date. The express purpose of section 63 of the Criminal Justice and Public Order Act 1994 is in fact, formally, to regulate gatherings 'on land in the open air of 100 or more persons . . . at which amplified music is played during the night . . . [and] is likely to cause serious distress to the inhabitants of the locality'. Section 64 gives supplementary powers of entry and seizure to the police, section 65 gives powers to stop persons proceeding to such a 'rave' and section 66 announces powers of the court to forfeit sound equipment. The question which this book seeks to answer is how, and how far, did the regulation of youth culture in the late 1970s, 1980s and 1990s − which culminated in the eventual criminalization of certain kinds of music − produce new (youth) cultures? For instance, are we now in an age of club rather than subcultures? Further, the book investigates the ways in which contemporary forms of popular culture (such as pop music and soccer) have developed in the context of a series of moral panics over 'deviant' folk devils in their midst during the last twenty years.

'Subculture to Clubcultures' is a pregnant phrase coined in the course of my work on the regulation of youth culture over three decades. It is meant to suggest the complexity of a cultural condition which has too often been reduced to one dimension (a fault which this author also exhibits!): for instance, the 'Old Left' cries of 'postmodernism' and 'Toryism' (hence, Major or Thatcher's children), or, as conservative sociologist Digby Anderson (Anderson, 1996) and his 'New Right' colleagues have it, 'the decline of manners'. The astute 'New Labour' commentator, David Marquand, has argued convincingly (Marquand and Seldon, 1996) that the phase of post-war society in Britain from the mid-1980s to the 1990s was one of 'hedonistic individualism', following a 'moralistic individualist' period in the late 1970s and early 1980s. Most of the chapters in this book, after initially setting the scene of regulation of youth culture in the moralistic individualism associated with the first five years of Margaret Thatcher's reign, report from the 'law and popular culture' front on the unfolding hedonistic individualism associated with her later rule and John Major's entire period of office, and the complex, unfolding repercussions up until the mid-1990s. They present a multiplicity of snapshots and criss-crossed narratives, adding up to a detailed contemporary picture of the recent history of regulating youth culture between 1979 and the present day.

PART I
SUBCULTURE

1 The Politics of Soccer Hooliganism

The 1978–9 English soccer season has just got under way with the headlines of the popular press screaming to the nation that a 'soccer hooligan' had been given a three-year prison sentence for committing 'grievous bodily harm'. The sporting bureaucrats, such as Harold Thompson of the Football Association, have been quoted as supporting judges' 'hardline' policy, and a working party on soccer violence, chaired by Labour's Sports Minister Dennis Howell, seems likely to continue to institutionalize such reaction. This follows the provisions in the Criminal Law Act 1977 for a massive increase in maximum fines for certain common law offences, almost universally seen by the media as a specific attack on soccer hooligans.

It seems that the Labour government is set on 'cleaning up' the game once and for all. Not only is terrace violence again being symbolically outlawed from the soccer scene, but the implementation of the new legislation on safety at sports grounds is having the effect of improving conditions for the stand-dweller and forcing those on the terraces to look even more like caged-up animals than they did before. The 'official' explanation for soccer hooliganism, as perpetuated in government reports and media discussions and 'enforced' at ground level by the police, reflects this inhuman environment. The 'reason' for soccer hooliganism, in this explanation, is that they are animals. Soccer hooliganism, as one pundit recently put it, is 'an entirely irrational collective spasm – animal instinct or the uncontrollable impulse of the insane'.

Reactions to such violence and vandalism increasingly take the form of more caging and more herding of 'the animals'. It has produced a predictable result – increased hooliganism. The police and the courts have thus become an integral part of the production of the 'social problem' of soccer hooliganism, the 'British disease', which must be stamped out at all costs. The solution has inevitably been largely to ignore 'liberal' reports such as that recently produced jointly by the Sports Council and the Social Science Research Council, and instead to recommend even stiffer sentences for soccer hooliganism.

Moral panics like this have become an everyday feature of life in Britain in the 1950s, 1960s and 1970s. However, the activity about which they generate public anxiety is not just a figment of the collective imagination of the media, courts and police. It *is* real, although, as we have seen, the official reaction to it cannot be ignored. With soccer hooliganism, even more than in the case of the scares about mods and rockers, teds, punks and so on, the historical and social context of the behaviour is crucial to really understanding it.

As many writers have pointed out, the history of professional soccer is largely a saga of one of the very few institutions which could be seen to involve mass working-class participation and control in the nineteenth century being progressively taken over by large and small middle-class entrepreneurs. This development – extending as it has into the late twentieth century – in itself, of course, does not account for soccer hooliganism. Soccer violence is, though, often explained in relation to an expression of the frustrations felt by (mainly) working-class youth as a result of such control in other areas of social life: for example, at work. Neither does the historical development account for the distinctly fascistic aspect to the 'resistance' on the terraces. We only need to think of recent recruitment campaigns by the National Front among soccer fans to realize that, as with other features of policing modern youth culture, the politics of youth are not simply to be read off from history. Soccer hooligans are not in any fundamental sense mere fodder for the right, nor are they manifestations of a spontaneous working-class collective resistance movement, as some on the left have seen them. Yet soccer does remain one of the relatively few areas of social life where working-class participation – if no longer control – remains high. The class background of most fans, players, managers and coaches is quite distinct from that of the tycoons who own and control the professional game. Most British soccer clubs are controlled by the chieftains of local industry and commerce in the towns where the clubs play, and the contrast is even starker when the class composition of the governing bodies of the game is examined.

In the 1970s, soccer has taken its place as one of the major leisure industries, not necessarily as profit making in itself, but certainly as an expensive and passive spectator sport in which the supporter has no real direct contact with the players or management (in a sense, still the historical 'representatives' of working-class fans) and even less with the administrators. Yet the illusion of contact – if not control – still persists. Soccer hooligans *identify* with their club; they fight for it, even though it publicly disowns them when they come up against the law. In contemporary cultural studies explanations, this is a 'magical' way of expressing collective ownership which takes the form of fighting, smashing up property and 'taking' other teams' supporters. However, as one recent piece of writing on Arsenal fans put it:

> You belong to the North Bank in so far as the North Bank belongs to you. But the North Bank is not owned by the kids or their parents or the organisations of their community, but by Dennis Hill-Wood, Chairman of the Arsenal Board of Directors, who sits on the Boards of 32 other companies. In the long run no-one can magically appropriate what in reality does not belong to them by virtue of their working class place in society. The pathos and futility of fighting amongst rival groups of socially dispossessed youth is the best demonstration of the extent of the victory of those who really do hold class power over them.

It is in this context that we need to view the recent hardening of official attitudes through the means of the law. The Anti-Nazi League's initiative in trying to organize the 'warriors on the terraces' is a welcome beginning, but it is currently the Labour government which is perpetuating the myth that soccer hooliganism has nothing to do with being a 'loyal supporter'. It is at the level of legislation and policy making that the campaign for democratic control of soccer urgently needs to be considered.

2 Keeping Off the Grass?

On Saturday, 9 March 1985, Garry Richardson interviewed Fenton Bresler, legal correspondent of the *Daily Mail*, for BBC Radio 2's *Sport on 2* programme. The interview followed trouble at Chelsea Football Club in the previous week, where an irate Chelsea fan had attacked Sunderland's Clive Walker, a former Chelsea 'hero', and various other disorders had occurred on and off the pitch at Stamford Bridge. Bresler, who just happens to have a flat overlooking the ground, began his diatribe by defending the law against the myriad criticisms of it emanating from diverse sections of opinion over the Walker incident. Bresler argued that the prosecution of the fan concerned under the Justices of the Peace Act 1361, which limited magistrates' powers of sentence to binding over, was mistaken and that all problems could have been averted if police had prosecuted under the Public Order Act 1936, which on breach of the peace charges would have given the same magistrates power to fine the offender up to £2,000. But the matter of soccer and the law did not end there. The distinguished correspondent proceeded to tell Richardson and the listeners some homespun truths: namely (to paraphrase), players' behaviour at professional soccer matches incites the crowd; fouls at professional matches all over the country every Saturday include many forms of behaviour which are 'illegal'; there is no reason why a soccer ground should be a sacred place free from the law; and furthermore, until someone is killed in professional soccer in Britain in such an incident, the necessary 'get tough' policy by the police and magistrates would not be forthcoming.

What is the background to media interventions into professional soccer – such as Fenton Bresler's – which along with changing practices in the police force and in soccer's governing bodies have helped to construct professional soccer in Britain as a key 'site' of social policy? The present Thatcher government's second 'task force'[1] is predictably organized to combat the 'enemy within', which is perceived to be using soccer matches as an excuse for hooligan disorder. The soccer *field* is thus literally a major object of inquiry in the 1980s. But where does this concern come from? Has the 'field' of soccer got a history? What does such a history tell us about the nature of legal regulation of, and intervention in, popular culture?

In many ways, we are now experiencing a crisis in the regulation (by legal and other means) of popular leisure similar to the upheavals witnessed in the early days of professional soccer in the nineteenth century. But the origins of the present crisis are in fact much more recent. The combination of the ending of the maximum wage in 1961, the granting of a modified form of 'freedom of contract' after the George Eastham court case in 1963,[2] and England's victory in the World Cup in 1966 may not have constituted the 'revolution' which was claimed for them, but they most certainly did usher in a new set of conditions through which the 'glory game' could be dragged screaming into the late twentieth century. Through the next twenty years there is a growing realization in the hallowed corridors of soccer clubs, Football League and Football Association, not to mention lawyers' offices and the heads of some chief constables, that something like the scenario that Fenton Bresler articulated for *Sport on 2* listeners was correct.

Why the Kissing Had to Stop

The exact nature of the relationship between players' on-the-field behaviour and spectator disorder has long been the subject of speculation. Journalists such as Arthur Hopcraft,[3] Jeff Powell[4] and Hugh McIlvanney[5] have all argued at one time or another that unruly action on the soccer field incites soccer hooliganism off it. However, assertion is no proof and there is plenty of quasi-sociological speculation arguing that there is no direct causal relation between what players do and fan behaviour. The *perception* that such cause exists, nevertheless, is what counts. When Mel Blyth remonstrated with his own goalkeeper at Colchester at the beginning of the 1980s, or, in an earlier phase, Sammy Nelson and Terry Mancini dropped their shorts as a gesture to their faithless followers, concern by police and soccer authorities was expressed in terms of their potentially detrimental effects on the terraces, not merely for the 'offence' the behaviour was seen to constitute *per se*.

The culmination of such concerns was played out on television screens in November 1983, when in a 'live' game the referee Clive Thomas pulled apart celebrating West Ham players who had just scored a goal against Manchester United. A few months later came statements from the Union of European Football Associations (UEFA) about 'wild celebrations' by players in European club and national championships, again widely witnessed as a result of the medium of television. Under the headline 'Scorers warned: cut the touchline antics or else', Bert Millichip, the chairman of the Football Association and a well-known hardliner on punishment, was quoted as saying:

> It is time . . . ridiculous antics . . . were stamped out. Of course, we are not against players celebrating and showing their feelings, but what we are concerned about is that they keep their standards of behaviour within acceptable limits. At the moment we are well beyond those limits . . . Spectators pay money to watch football, not to see players showering each other with kisses every time a goal is scored. These antics destroy the dignity of football and we are determined that they should stop.

Millichip also revealed in this newspaper interview with the *Mail on Sunday* that the Football Association had sent letters to all Football League clubs six weeks earlier requesting co-operation to prevent 'excessive over-exuberance'.

In fact this '1984' (*sic*) campaign is reminiscent of a similar project, conducted simultaneously by the Federation of International Football Associations (FIFA), which attempted to ban 'outbursts of emotion' on the field. This was led by the Football Association and occurred only three years earlier, in the 'notorious' 1980–1 soccer season. The Football Association had issued a sixteen-point memorandum to Football League clubs in order, it was asserted, 'to help improve the game's image and cool tempers on the terraces'. Among many other recommendations it stated that excessive shows of exuberance when goals are scored should be discouraged, and specifically called for players to stop running to the crowd in jubilation when they had scored a goal; furthermore, the Football Association wanted to eliminate arm-waving and fist-clenching poses. On many of the matters contained in the document relating to players' conduct, the Football Association drew on itself nothing but ridicule and contempt – especially among players themselves. One north-west club captain and Professional Footballers' Association representative whom I interviewed told me how the notice from the old, austere body had been pinned on the board at the club and over the weeks curled up at the edges, unreadable and, he suspected, unread – an apt symbol of the players' regard for the style of Football Association intervention in such matters.

Farcical though these attempts at regulation 'from above' in the soccer industry may appear to be – and, let it be noted, generally unsuccessful too – there is a more serious point to them. The Football Association and the Football League have for a hundred years attempted similar action, at various times and in various guises. Professional soccer players' behaviour has *always* been minutely scrutinized and subjected to surveillance by the powers that be (or would like to be). Such scrutiny has frequently depended on no other criteria than the particular social mores of the time and the group enforcing the decisions: for instance, the 'amateur gentlemen' of the Football Association in the 1890s, or whatever collection of butchers, candlestick-makers and assorted professional men happened to make up the numbers in the Football League in the postwar world. What is distinct about the new regulation instituted by such bodies is the context of the enforcement of such prejudices. Two in particular seem to me to be important; again Bresler perhaps inadvertently put his legal finger on them. They are the question of conduct on the field constituting (or otherwise) illegalities, that is to say breaches of civil or criminal law and not merely breaches of Football Association or Football League rule books; and the question of the encroachment of the law into the 'private' space of the soccer ground.

Unprofessional Fouls

In 1983 there occurred an out-of-court settlement of the first civil court action in *professional* soccer in Britain involving one player suing another for injuries inflicted during a game. Jim Brown, former Scottish international and Dunfermline Athletic captain, claimed £30,000 damages over a tackle by John Pelosi of St Johnstone in a game between the respective clubs in October 1981. Brown sustained a broken leg as a result of the tackle and subsequently sued Pelosi and, as his employer, St Johnstone Football Club. Pelosi had already been banned for the remainder of the relevant soccer season, having been sent off for the late tackle on Brown at the time. The terms of the settlement were not disclosed and of course the legal arguments were never put to the test in open court. As a Scottish case it would not have been binding on English courts, but the settlement, widely reported in the press, caused Gordon Taylor, the secretary of the Professional Footballers' Association, to state:

> There are many implications in the Scottish case and it is a salutary lesson for all players . . . There have been one or two unsavoury incidents on occasion, and I think it might be an opportune time to give our members a further warning . . . Every year I warn all our members that they not only have to abide by the rules of the game but they also have to abide by the law.

All kinds of speculation can be made as a result of the Brown case. Would English courts have upheld Brown's claim for damages against a fellow professional? Indeed, would the Edinburgh Court of Session have done so if it had not been denied the opportunity to hear the case? How important was it that Brown's long and relatively distinguished career in professional soccer was brought to an abrupt and comparatively early end (he was only 31 at the time of his final game) by the offending tackle? Would the legal response be qualitatively different if a player only had to suffer a spell of reserve team soccer as a result of 'illegal' tackling?

What is interesting from a popular cultural perspective, however, is the specific climate which this case helped to create, and yet which it also followed in the wake of. The same newspaper article which reported the comments of Gordon Taylor inferred that an English Football League player, Derrick Parker, was in the process of considering taking out similar action in the courts after an incident involving Mick McCarthy, then of Barnsley FC, which had occurred at the previous Saturday's fixture between Parker's former club, Barnsley, and his present club, Oldham Athletic. Rumour and counter-rumour of domestic scandal surrounding Parker's stay at Barnsley abounded in the days after the incident, and in the end no legal action resulted.

However, prior to the announcemnt of a settlement of the Brown case, the 1980s had already had its share of 'unsavoury' incidents on the pitch. To cite just one at random, in February 1982 Gerry Gow, a renowned 'hard man' just signed from Manchester City, welcomed the visitors (Derby County) to Rotherham by gashing the shin of an apponent, Barry Powell, in the first minute. Gow was booked, a free kick was given and from the restart Gow tackled Derby's Steve Emery, who suffered a badly broken leg. Gow then retired for the proverbial (very) early bath. No court case resulted on this occasion either.

Up until the 1984–5 season, tactics had seemingly been to accept the Brown case as a symbolic warning of what might occur. Parker, Emery and many others simply, for whatever complex of personal reasons, decided to adopt a *laissez-faire* – leave alone, or 'keep off the grass' – approach. The only legalistic interventions have been through the normal machinery of the discipline bodies of soccer's governing authorities. So we currently do not know what an English court would make of a civil action involving claims for damages as a result of incidents on the field of play.

Two recent incidents are significant, nevertheless, in that their seriousness may still prompt action in the courts, Both involved the sending off of the offending player and in both the 'victim' was carried off with a broken leg. Jeff Hopkins of Fulham was sent off after fouling David Burke of Huddersfield, who suffered a leg fracture in the fixture between the clubs on 23 March 1985; and Henry Hughton of Crystal Palace was sent off on 2 April after a foul, much publicized and condemned in the press, on Gerry Ryan of Brighton, who also sustained a badly broken leg. It is probably still too early to say whether legal action will be prompted in either or both cases.

What has also occurred, however, in the 1984–5 season is a distinct change of strategy. Dennis Mortimer of Aston Villa initiated a unique disciplinary case when he deliberately turned away from the courts and brought the first private complaint by one professional footballer against another under Football Association disciplinary machinery. When on loan to Sheffield United, Barnsley's Roger Wylde is alleged to have injured Mortimer in an off-the-ball incident in the fixture between the clubs on 23 February 1985. Mortimer was carried off with a lip wound which necessitated six stitches, and he claimed that Wylde had simply struck him in the face with deliberate intent. The Football Association rule in question prohibits 'insulting or improper behaviour or acting in a manner likely to bring the game into disrepute'. Although the Football Association commission accepted that Mortimer had received a serious facial injury, it held that there was not enough evidence to provoke disciplinary action against Wylde. Even after this, however, Mortimer was not going to turn to the law courts. He was quoted in the media as proclaiming: 'I shall not take it to a civil court. I wanted to keep this within the realms of our profession.'

This tendency to revert to the procedures set up by soccer's governing bodies may well be a pointer to the future for professional players. After all, court cases are notoriously costly and uncertain. Elsewhere, though, there are signs that legal encroachments on to the soccer field are not so easily reversed.

Policing the Field

As if to serve as a reminder of certain relations in the industry and to emphasize the encroachment on the 'private' sphere of soccer clubs of the 'public' regulatory forces of police and law courts, the 1980s opened with a rush of prosecutions, and threats of prosecutions, for public order and other, criminal offences *on the field* of play. Not that 'public' intervention, through police and courts, on the players' playing terrain is unheard of in the history of professional soccer in England and Wales. For example, from the early period of professionalism in the late nineteenth century there are records of a number of cases of legal regulation of players' behaviour. Moreover, this tendency of players to be involved in disturbances, of course, is not simply confined to on-the-field behaviour, but it is certainly the playing side which has recently come to be the focus of attention of academic lawyers, law enforcement agencies and the soccer authorities themselves.

It had not, until the 1980–1 season, been a general practice of the civil authorities to bring charges against players who 'misbehave' on the field. This is not to argue that there were no earlier attempts to do so. If we look back to the 1950s, for instance, Tim Ward,[6] then manager of Barnsley FC, recalled that when any opposition player was sent off for violent conduct a policeman would approach the manager, out of courtesy, after the game to see if there was a desire on the part of the player on the receiving end to bring assault charges against the sent-off player. In fact, Ward always refused to allow the policeman to see the player concerned. It may well have been paternalism, born of the 'soccer slavery' era, which prompted such managerial action, and it would indeed be interesting in this context to know how widespread such practices were in the 1950s and 1960s.

The same manager tells of one perhaps even more surprising legal intervention in a slightly earlier period when he was a player in a postwar game in Manchester. After one of his Derby County colleagues had hit a spectator when leaving the field at half-time – a telling reminder, incidentally, that on-the-field behaviour can often involve spectator/player/coach/official conflict as well as player versus player – two policemen immediately came into the dressing room of the away team to arrest the player. In the event, the player continued with the second half of the game as his team-mates were not exactly forthcoming when the policemen required clear evidence of the assault. But the soccer governing bodies have frequently been reminded that when one player attacks another with fists or feet, or alternatively, attacks an official, then the action amounts to the criminal offence of assault.

The very great increase in televised soccer, enabling such offences to be witnessed by millions of viewers, has in the last two decades moved politicians and law officers to warn soccer authorities that, unless they took effective steps to discipline players and prevent such incidents, the time could come when those responsible for administering the criminal law might have to step in. This is effectively what happened at the beginning of the 1980–1 season when there was a veritable spate of interventions by individual policemen against players' on-the-field behaviour. As sports law barrister and author Edward Grayson has put it in the *Rothman's Year Book*:

> the season ended almost as it began. The minority disgrace of England's supporters at Basle on the occasion of the end-of-season international against Switzerland threw the mind back to the opening explosions of violence both on and off the field at its commencement. Vince Hilaire of Crystal Palace pushed over a referee and was found guilty by a disciplinary tribunal of bringing the game into disrepute. Charlie George of Southampton was disciplined by his club and fined by local magistrates for assaulting a photographer at the Norwich City ground; and the law and sport merged dramatically when a police officer marched onto the field at Colchester to remonstrate about a defender's verbal chastisement of his own goalkeeper. This occasion was not without precedent. In the late 1960s a visiting player at Portsmouth made rude signs during a FA cup tie which could have incited crowd disturbances. A local policeman, on that occasion, attemped to object too. Each time the referee complained, but forgot how the law of the land transcends the field of play;

and both referees could have been at risk for obstructing the respective police officers in the execution of their duty.

As a result of one of the incidents, Charlie George, a former England international, then of Southampton (and famed for his elevation from the North Bank terraces to a popular player at Arsenal), was fined £400 for hitting a press photographer in a game against Norwich City in September 1980. George admitted threatening behaviour likely to cause breach of the peace.

This increased surveillance and regulation of players' behaviour on the pitch was not *simply* the result of a few 'over-zealous' policemen; it was part of a programme of wider regulation of the behaviour of professional players, and, crucially, soccer supporters. Police spokesmen have joined the fray, and despite the general danger of a flood of unwarranted legal cases,[7] there have been stern warnings that soccer players who break the law on the pitch could be taken to court.[8] In 1982 South Yorkshire's chief constable issued a three-point guideline to players in his region which said: 'Don't provoke spectators; don't show dissent; play the game in the proper spirit.' He warned that 'if players break the law, they will be taken to court' and that those 'who misbehave but don't commit a crime would also be in trouble as they would be reported to their clubs and police would ask for disciplinary action'. This is by no means a 1980s phenomenon, however. A marked example of the beginning of such a campaign of surveillance within the game was as far back as 1974 at the biennial congress of UEFA held in Edinburgh. The congress resolved to 'intensify their campaign against indiscipline by players and spectators'. At the same time John McCluskey QC, the Solicitor-General for Scotland, gave a warning that, unless soccer authorities put their house in order, prosecutions for criminal assault, following incidents on the field, would be inevitable.

In 1975, after much discussion following the Wheatley Report[9] on crowd safety in 1972 (itself the result of the disaster at Ibrox Park, Glasgow in 1971), the Safety of Sports Grounds Act 1975 passed through Parliament. The effect of this legislation and its guidelines[10] – though ostensibly confined to licensing of soccer grounds on safety criteria – was to contribute to the continuing process of redefining the soccer audience from predominantly skilled working class to (more) middle class.[11] The law aided the increased surveillance by ordinary and 'elite' police squads (for instance, the Tactical Aid Group (TAG) in Greater Manchester) and closed-circuit television (where operated) of supporters *within and around* the grounds. Difficulties have been experienced with the content and scope of the legislation, but it is clear that this apparently 'innocent' law has been a crucial force behind the movement in the late 1970s and 1980s to segregate and monitor one section of the English soccer crowd – that is, the terraces. It is a process which is now seen as part of the repackaging of soccer, remarketing it for a non-'hooligan' audience, as Jimmy Hill, former chairman of Coventry City, has recently put it. Hill's own solution at Coventry City, which was to institute the first all-seater stadium in the Football League, has backfired somewhat.[12]

The debate about segregating terrace supporters had been in motion for some time before the 1975 Act was passed: for example, Denis Howell, the then Labour government's Minister of Sport, urged in 1974 that soccer terraces be split into sections to stop hooligans getting on the pitch. Howell chaired the government working party on crowd safety in this period, and the legislation undoubtedly followed from such considerations. It was not merely safety that was at issue: the behaviour of spectators on the terraces was seen to be in urgent need of regulation. 'Architectural' solutions, including the speeding up of the provision of all-seater stadiums, were widely propagated in 1974 and 1975. The Act appeared as a 'natural' outcome of 'sensible' discussions about 'rioters' at soccer grounds.

It was Manchester United 'soccer hooligans', in particular, who became more than mere 'folk devils' around which moral panics were created, and who came to play a significant part in the drama of policing soccer in contemporary Britain in the late 1970s and 1980s. Their highly publicized invasion of the pitch after a home game with Manchester City in April 1974 – which caused the game to be abandoned and, since Manchester United was losing, confirmed that the home team was to be relegated to Division 2 – was the occasion for renewed calls for 'seats for rioters', and demonstrated clearly that the pitch invaders were a large minority, were easily identifiable and 'normally monopolise specific areas of the ground'. By 1976, with Margaret Thatcher installed as opposition leader, it was common for news-papers to call for the return of corporal punishment and for ticket bans as specific solutions to the problem of Manchester United's 'hooliganism element', and soccer violence in general.

Of course, Manchester United 'soccer hooligans' were not the only figures in the public debate about vandalism and violence in the 1970s – Spurs fans' exploits in Rotterdam in May 1974 in the second leg of the UEFA Cup Final and Glasgow Rangers supporters' 'friendly' trip to Aston Villa in October 1976 earned them a notoriety which was matched only by the fans of Millwall, Chelsea and Leeds United in later years. However, such figures are social constructions of a highly mediated kind. As Garry Whannel (1979) has argued in conclusion to a rigorous account of the mass media treatment of soccer hooliganism in Britain:

> The structuring process of public discussion has constructed two figures around which the debate is formed: *the football hooligan* and the *family audience*. The hooligan took its place within an increasingly formalised mode of expla-nation; the label *hooligan* came to reference a whole section of the terrace sub-culture.

The notion of the 'family audience' makes full sense only if it is understood to reference the affluent middle-class consumer. The presence in development plans of squash courts, hairdressing salons, executive boxes and expensive restaurants indicates that soccer clubs are increasingly looking to the top end of their market for economic salvation. As Whannel points out: 'What is significant here for the concept of deviance labelling is that the folk devil *soccer hooligan* does not simply become part of a law-enforcement induced amplification as a figure in a more general discourse, the real basis of which remains unspoken.'

In fact, the more general 'discourse' proved to be part of a larger process of regulation of both players and spectators, in which the soccer authorities, clubs and mass media, especially, could be seen as redefining the audience for soccer. This process of redefinition of the soccer audience by the mass media has been seen to occur specifically in television, but in my view it is the practices of the law itself and consequent enforcement by clubs and police which have had the major effect in the development of surveillance of terrace culture. It has contributed to the 'caging' of (sub)cultures, particularly the younger element, by penning them in, thus making it easier for surveillance and regulation to take place. Much police removal of alleged 'provocateurs' is quite arbitrary, made considerably easier since the enactment of the 1975 legislation by the smaller terrace area created. Further, legislation in Scotland – the Criminal Justice (Scotland) Act 1980 – extended surveillance of supporters to such an extent that it is now an offence to carry drink or alcohol on a coach travelling to or from a sporting event, or to attempt to enter a ground drunk or in possession of alcohol.

The extention of such laws to England and Wales in the near future can in no way be ruled out,[13] especially in the light of the Football Association's frequently expressed intention to regulate (including banning entirely) the sale of alcohol to soccer supporters. This process of copying the measures already adopted in Scotland in the early 1980s has been speeded up by the direct government intervention immediately after the Luton versus Millwall FA Cup game on 13 March 1985, where soccer hooliganism was subject to all the paraphernalia usually associated with TV coverage of sport in the 1980s (action replays, slow motion, etc.), not to mention the predictable press outrage and the equally predictable calls from various quarters for matches to be banned.[14] The difference in this particular initiative to combat 'the enemy within' is the cajoling of a rather reluctant Football Association to toe the Thatcher government's distinctly hard line on 'offenders', echoed not surprisingly by the *Daily Mail*'s legal correspondent, Fenton Bresler, in the radio interview quoted earlier, only days before the Luton versus Millwall 'riots' took place.

The now notorious episode of Chelsea's installation of an electric fence at Stamford Bridge[15] merely illustrates the limits of the Thatcher government's 'get tough' policies on law and order in general, and soccer hooliganism in particular. The likely short–term outcome of the current debate is a change in Football Association rule 31, making clubs themselves more *legally* responsible for what happens on the terrace than under present regulations which only require them to take 'all reasonable precautions'. However, the question of whether government (in its widest sense) should 'keep off the grass' is not simply a matter of 'public' regulation, operating through criminal and civil law, coming together with 'private' regulation by clubs, Football Association and League. Talk of public regulation of private activity in this context is merely confusing the issue.

Recently, the English judiciary has also involved itself in this kind of misleading discourse, establishing that soccer stadiums would be endowed, by judicial edict, with the label 'public places',[16] and furthermore, that private control over such public places would extend to the granting of injunctions to soccer clubs restraining those who are banned from the ground as a result of disturbances from entering until the club sees fit.[17] The development of legal intervention in this (soccer) field is rapidly coming to reflect the more general 'free–market, strong–state' solutions that are so characteristic of the Thatcher government, and which have wreaked so much havoc in the fabric of British society in the 1980s.

3 The Soccer War

It was entirely predictable that soccer hooligans would be 1985's 'enemy within' for the Thatcher government; what better alien force for the Iron Lady to take on after vanquishing the 'Argies' and the miners? Soccer louts would be an easy and popular prize for a law and order government, the completion of an historic treble. Set up a 'war cabinet', encourage the further development of a National Reporting Centre style of policing operation, headed by a tough, right-wing police chief like James Anderton, and reap an electoral harvest. That was the battle plan. But the war will be something else. And the casualties will include civil liberties as well as professional soccer in Britain as we have known them for at least the last twenty years.

Part of the difficulty for Margaret Thatcher is that, though her second task force is already dispatched, the hooligans themselves, especially when setting foot on foreign shores, are celebrating precisely the mix of values which made up the Falklands spirit in 1982. A tough, traditional brand of masculinity, proven by combat; a clear, racist superiority over other nations and their cultures; above all, a sense of being British or, even more pointedly, English, with all the mythology of past 'glories' which that brings. Truly the bulldog breed. The problem is that the Falklands task force style is almost indistinguishable from that of the newly discovered enemy within.

More than this, it is possible to see in the styles of national and club sides, and the language of managers, coaches and administrators, this fresh conception of Englishness and the remaking of the English working class in the image of colonial adventure. It is almost twenty years since Alf Ramsey described the Argentinians as 'animals' after their infamous World Cup match with England at Wembley. But there has been plenty more chauvinist claptrap where that came from whenever post-Ramsey English team managers have opened their mouths. The language of battle and armies is seemingly over-present, underscored by commentators' own Coleman-balls vocabulary, and teams' styles (with a few notable exceptions) display an obsession with hard-working 'professional' attitudes to the exclusion of soccer 'magic' – the skilful, stylish player who can turn a game in a split second, but do nothing for the rest of the ninety minutes. Is it coincidence that twenty years on from England's World Cup triumph, when Jimmy Greaves was shamefully shunned, a player like Glen Hoddle, or even Trevor Francis, is still 'on trial'? Even more pertinently, the famous soccer cliché about black players not having the 'bottle' is being tested on a national stage. The recent prediction of an all-black England soccer team by 1990 is starting to look tattered with the constant undermining by the media and 'experts' of the staying power of flair players like John Barnes, despite his 'Brazilian'-style goal in the Maracana stadium last year. It is as if the white, less than masculine players, such as Hoddle, are not quite English and would be better off plying their wares abroad; which fits very nicely with the overt, organized racism at many matches, particularly England games in the 1980s, when the equation is black equals skilful.

Football 'hooliganism', of course, has been around for as long as the rest of the game itself – in its professional form at least. But the 1980s lads are clearly 'Thatcher's boys', just as prostitutes from north of Watford are 'Thatcher's girls'. In the depths of recession, selling sex as a commodity in the market place is an understandable aspect of a 'survival culture'. Similarly, the worst-hit geographical areas of Britain have predictably witnessed a backlash of aggressive masculinity, notable Merseyside, Manchester, south and west Yorkshire, and the north-east. Anfield has been no place for the faint-hearted – and I don't mean just opposition teams – for a good few years now. The media myth of loveable scousers singing witty songs on the Kop is just as dated as Gerry Marsden's remake of 'You'll never walk alone'. Hence the hooligan-inspired Brussels tragedy – though not, of course, its scale – could have been expected sooner or later. There's been plenty of practice for it at home, and occasionally abroad, over recent seasons.

But this is not the whole story. If it were, Thatcher's version of events would strike home much deeper. The soccer fans of the 1980s who stir up trouble on the terraces (and stands and shopping centres) are even more her children. The rise of the casuals and their association with some of the most (loosely) organized soccer ground violence is a caricature of the 'affluent' eighties: as Simon Frith has called it, 'bullying clothed in respectability'. How ironic that it has been soccer stadiums, most of them crumbling (or burning) into decay, which have witnessed the array of expensive sports and menswear in this fashion-conscious decade – some of it bought with the proceeds of looting. These have been (life)style wars with a vengeance.

The left has always had problems with explaining, or organizing around, soccer hooliganism. Either it has seen the fighting crews and their fellow travellers as expressions of traditional working-class resistance to the 'embourgeoisement' of the game, or it has simply condemned them as fascist louts. Both of these are caricatures. An inability to move beyond such analyses has laid out a fallow field for Thatcher. But identity cards, bans on alcohol, increased surveillance through video and the like may only succeed in further displacing the trouble from the terraces to the streets. Many of the top First Division grounds have long been so strictly monitored and segregated (and it was Labour's Dennis Howell who was responsible for the introduction of 'caging' of fans, so don't expect any liberal solutions there!) that they are like top-security prisons with few escapees. If Margaret Thatcher and her free-market gang have their way, there will probably be only these clubs left before this century is out, and the increasingly desperate battle of 'barmy armies' will be taking place elsewhere.

4 Thatcher's Boys (Next Door)

The soccer hooligan has emerged once more in 1985 to claim pride of place, like his ancestors, in the public folk devil hall of fame. In the season 1984–5, Millwall caused mayhem at Luton, Chelsea at Sunderland and Leeds at Birmingham. Via the Heysel stadium Liverpool outdid them all, gaining European and world recognition in a manner that the team, for all its glory, had never achieved. The 'scousers' had surpassed all previous attempts by British soccer fans to stamp their authority on Europe once and for all. Leeds, Manchester United, Spurs, Celtic and Rangers had all tried, but it was only Liverpool who had a realistic chance of achieving the coveted goal. Their unrivalled record of continuous involvement in European competition stretches back to the early 1970s, and since that time the 'cheerful and witty scousers' had thieved and fought their way across Europe, bringing back the spoils of contest to Merseyside. The team had also done its part on the pitch, bringing back trophy after trophy.

The experience of previous seasons' hard campaigns stood team and supporters in good stead – cumulative experience on how to look after yourself on the continent and how to assert the pride of Merseyside. As a result Heysel was easy: dodgy fences, pathetic segregation and an incompetent police force. No one consciously meant for thirty-nine to die, but it would serve as a warning to rivals both at home and abroad: 'Are you watching, Manchester?'

'Heysel, Heysel 85, Heysel 85', will no doubt join 'Munich, Munich 58' in the chants next season, as well as

He's only a poor little wop,
His feathers all tattered and torn,

He made me feel sick, so I hit him with a brick,
And now he don't sing any more.

Liverpool had certainly outclassed the rest: 'the lads had done well'.

One thing that should have occurred to anyone watching the Heysel incident or the well-publicized events in England over the last year was the absence of the hooligan stereotype, the skinhead. This infamous folk devil who had stomped the terraces since the 1960s was nowhere to be seen. Instead, the public were treated to full frontal exposure of the new hooligan, quite different but clearly more dangerous in terms of the death and destruction he was causing, on the television screen.

The casual/scally/perry (depending on their city origin) has been sighted before, with various articles appearing in *The Face* and the popular papers as well as on Channel 4's *Earsay*. However, it wasn't until 'General' Muranyi and the 'soldiers' of Cambridge's 'Main Firm' were sentenced for periods ranging from fifteen months to five years for successfully ambushing Chelsea's 'Anti-Personnel Firm' that the media had to confront the new hooligan. Judge Hilliard described the 'General' as 'articulate' and 'fluent', and the media reported that this 'smartly dressed gang of thugs' wore 'Pringle jumpers, denims and training shoes to make them look more like the boy next door than soccer hooligans' (*Daily Mirror*).

However, the media did not think it worthwhile to explain the incongruence between their stereotype and the actual reality. Indeed, the *Mirror* seemed to be suggesting that the hooligans were trying to disguise themselves, rather than realizing that the 'General' and his 'soldiers' approximated the stereotype more closely than the skinhead.

In most cities over the past six years, there has been a proliferation of youth styles and fashions, each 'tribe' easily identifiable by its respective clothes, hairstyles and adornments. By comparison, one could also see very 'straight' styles being worn: t-shirts, straight jeans (or tracksuits) and a pair of trainers, as well as 'respectable' haircuts. At first sight, these young people looked like an undifferentiated mass, but nothing could be further from the truth. If you knew what to look for, you soon realized that these young people were engaged in style wars, the like of which had not been seen since the original 'mod' era of the 1960s. The difference is, of course, that the pesent style wars are taking place in the middle of a recession that is hitting young people very hard.

These youths have developed a style that is constantly changing in the quest to be more different and more exclusive. The Fred Perry t-shirts gave way to Adidas and then to the expensive labels like Tacchini, Fila and Lacoste. The small name motif on the shirt would mean nothing to most people, but to the casuals it signified how much it cost: between £15 for the cheap labels and £40 for a 'good' t-shirt, and between £50 and £120 for a 'good' tracksuit. The 'in' trainers ranged from Adidas to Nike and Puma, the 'wedge' haircut became longer at the back and front, and straight Lois and Levis jeans, in certain instances, gave way to flares. This rapidity of change has led to some casuals giving up sportswear and labels. It has also led to regional peculiarities and differences.

In Liverpool the 'scallies' have their own bands, particularly The Farm, and music/soccer fanzine, *The End*. *The End* is the forum where 'scallies', 'Mancs', 'Cockneys', etc. argue it out over who had what first. At the moment Armarni jumpers, Pink Floyd and Bob Dylan t-shirts are all in, as well as 'Manc' flares and the obligatory 'draw'. Last season also saw the final flowering of the now infamous ski and bobble hats, first of all in the colours of Everton and Liverpool. These were soon joined by ½ Everton ½ Celtic, ½ Everton ½ Rangers, ½ Liverpool ½ Celtic, ½ Liverpool ½ Rangers. Very soon Manchester and London followed, the predominance of ½ Celtic hats over ½ Rangers hats or vice versa being determined by the sectarian histories of the respective clubs. In addition, the 'scallies' began to sport continental, particularly German, ones as both Everton and Liverpool progressed towards their respective European finals.

Manchester casuals were responsible for the cord flares comeback, the logical conclusion to developments in their trouser styles over the past few years. First, narrow jeans were slit at the bottom of each seam to allow them to lie on the trainer, and tracksuit bottoms were worn with the side zips undone for the same effect. Both gave the impression of flares at the bottom of the trousers, so the next step was actually to wear flare-bottomed cords. Consequently, shops in Manchester have all been cashing in on this style. Manchester and Liverpool casuals have also shared a liking for long baggy jumpers, this rivalry going back to 1979–80, as well as 'sheepies' in the winter, the more expensive the better.

The London casuals claim to have given up sportswear, first moving on to the top menswear shops selling Burberry macs, Chester Barrie suits, Farrah slacks, Daks and croc shoes. Toby Young reported in the *Observer* in June 1985 that north London casuals were wearing 'long flowery paisley shirts, with the top buttons done up, fastened with diamante broaches and the tails hanging out over Pepe jeans and Farrah slacks'. However, their south London Chelsea counterparts 'go for soft, beige light combinations'. Although each city has developed its own unique traits, each influencing the other, the overall emphasis is on very expensive style, the Rolex watches and gold chains accompanying the clothes. The competition is intense, with acute rivalry over who is most stylish.

So, where does soccer hooliganism enter into this quest for style? For groups of these young casuals, soccer is as central to their lives as it has always been to working-class male life. It is possible to argue that the central concerns of the casuals have been responsible for their particular type of soccer violence, witnessed during recent seasons. Allied to the casuals has been the emergence of the various inter-city 'fighting crews' connected with soccer clubs. Every club has a named 'crew', Leeds United's 'Service Crew'; West Ham United's 'Inter-City Firm'; Chelsea's 'Anti-Personnel Firm'; Millwall's 'Bushwackers'; Manchester City's 'Maine Line Crew'; Portsmouth's '6.57 Crew'; Cambridge's 'Main Firm', and many more. Whether these 'crews' actually exist in the same form as, for example, the various New York and Los Angeles ethnic street gangs is questionable. As Martyn Harris pointed out in *New Society* in 1982, with regard to Leeds, the names used depend upon which journalist the young fans happen to be talking to. What does matter is that they have a recognized name to cover their actions when clashing with rival supporters.

The above names originate with the supporters who travel not as part of the official supporters' clubs, but in advance, on separate trains, in style. West Ham's 'Inter-City Firm' are supposed to travel to away games in first-class compartments, while Manchester City's 'Maine Line Crew' travel on the luxury inter-city coaches rather than the official club coaches. Allied to this is the propensity to travel by private car and minibus – this was the reason why Cambridge and Chelsea clashed so viciously.

Dressed very 'respectably', with no visible club identification or chanting, fans travelling in this manner can circumvent local policing measures laid on for the visiting official supporters' clubs. Consequently, there is the freedom to cause mayhem if they so wish. Liverpool fans, for example, took Manchester city centre by storm several seasons ago by arriving earlier than expected. Portsmouth police[1] have told the legendary story about how the '6.57 Crew' 'hired morning suits and had travelled to Cardiff by train, convincing the British Transport Police that they were to attend a wedding'. Travelling in style and comfort, a bizarre parody of 'the age of the train', means that these supporters can foil official attempts to control them.

Within the grounds, the competition over style reflects itself in taunts and chants. Regionalism has been given a sharp and vicious turn by the casuals. When Liverpool and Everton visit London, they are goaded about the poverty of Merseyside. The London casuals have flashed £5 to £10 notes in the same manner as the Metropolitan Police did during the miners' strike. Northern rivals also taunt the Merseyside teams as well:

In your Liverpool slums,
You look in the dustbin for something to eat,
You find a dead rat and you think it's a treat,
In your Liverpool slums.

More recently, additional insults have included:

Sign on, sign on with hope in your heart,
And you'll never get a job

and

One job between you,
You've only got one job between you.

Before, during and after the 1985 FA Cup Final, Everton and Manchester
United casuals taunted each other over who was the scruffiest. The miners'
strike also echoed in taunts throughout its duration. Manchester City fans,
when they played Yorkshire and Welsh teams, chanted: 'Arthur Scargill is a
wanker, is a wanker' and 'Get back to work you lazy twats'. They greeted
Nottingham's fans with 'You scab bastards, you scab bastards'. A bitter
regionalism that has always existed has been fuelled by the casual competition to be the best, a matching up of pride against pride. This is what the
soccer style wars are all about.

The buying of season tickets in the more expensive seating areas has also
been fashionable among young casuals (as has been the buying of seats when
away from home). Again, this involves the flaunting of cash, but there are
other good reasons for having a season ticket. It means that you don't have
to queue where the police pay most attention and you can turn up at the last
minute and gain access with little difficulty. As a result of previous official
responses to soccer hooliganism, most terraces are now heavily segregated
and policed. The only free space is to be found in the 'respectable' seating
areas where there is less segregation, less policing, easier access and greater
comfort. Over the last couple of seasons, young casuals have made some of
these seating areas their own, standing up and waving to fellow supporters
in other parts of the ground and to the cameras if present. Not content with
buying expensive seats, they must be seen to have bought them.

The consequence of rival fans laying claim to these seats is an inevitable
clash at some stage. As soon as the away casuals identify themselves by
chanting or directly attacking those about them, violence will erupt. Of
course, when the clashes happen the seats also make good weapons; they are
now the only form of weapon to be found inside the big soccer grounds.
Fans associated with Leeds and Manchester United have wrecked Coventry's
all-seater ground, which was supposed to be the solution to hooliganism. A
massive television audience witnessed Millwall supporters ripping up the
expensive seats at Luton to drive back the police. Chelsea also caused havoc
among the seating areas at Sunderland, once more using the seats as missiles.
In addition, these areas allow easier access to other parts of the ground and
provide easier exit routes to get at opposing fans outside the ground.

The casuals' emphasis on style has completely outwitted attempts to control soccer hooliganism. When going to away matches, the majority of supporters will be met and herded by the local police into the away cattlepens, where they will have to put up with the taunts of the home supporters. However, a minority will have travelled in style with little chance of detection, and will be able to enjoy half a pint, and if opposing fans are encountered there will be a realistic chance of getting at them. Gaining easy access to the home supporters' seating areas allows unlimited potential for trouble. At some stage they will identify themselves and attack, or wait for the home casuals to respond. The level of response by the latter is an indication, first, of whether they can afford to sit in their own ground, and second, of whether they are 'hard' enough to defend that ground. All those on the terraces can do is watch the clashes or provide vocal encouragement to those prepared to 'have a go'.

It is at this moment that the regional style wars, at their sharpest, take on the cutting edge of a Stanley knife, slashing through a rival expensive jumper, shirt or casual face. As the chant chillingly says: 'Ten men went to mow, went to mow at Chelsea'. Consequently, official responses such as Mr Justice Popplewell's interim report on Bradford City's fire disaster, with their calls for bans on away supporters and the introduction of identity cards, will not stop the casuals enjoying an 'away-day special'.

PART II
SUBCULTURE
INTO
CLUBCULTURE

5 The Rehabilitation of Soccer

For a change, in 1986 the European Cup Final was not contested by an English club team – not because Canon League Champions Everton were unsuccessful in earlier rounds of the competition, but as a result of the UEFA ban on all English clubs in European matches. Following Liverpool and other English fans' charges at the Heysel stadium in May 1985 – leading to the deaths of thirty-nine spectators, mostly Italian, as stadium walls collapsed – European hopefuls stayed at home to contest the Screen Sport Super Cup. Early next season the Merseyside rivals will no doubt go through the motions in the final of this 'Mickey Mouse' trophy, but the real action will be taking place on the playing fields of Europe.

Although FIFA quickly followed suit and imposed bans on English clubs playing anywhere abroad, the English national team is still free to play in the 1986 World Cup Finals in Mexico next month. Hoping against hope that there is no repeat of last year's tragedy at Heysel, or even the National Front's nasty little peep show in South America last summer, FA officials have been carefully plotting a route back on to the continent as soon as the period of national penance will allow, confident of avoiding a recurrence of bad publicity which might jeopardize England's participation in the 1988 European Championship. Liverpool chairman John Smith excepted, it is possible to detect over the past season a kind of reverse 'moral panic' in operation, a playing down of soccer's domestic troubles and a talking up of government measures to 'tackle' the problem.

It is now, twelve months on from Heysel, quite easy to forget what all the fuss was about. The Thatcher government has encountered new 'enemies within' – the printworkers, the prison officers, even 'disloyal' cabinet ministers – and the 'war' on soccer hooligans announced after the televised highlights of Millwall's invasion of Kenilworth Road, Luton in March 1985 has to some extent faded from public view. Those incidents which *have* received widespread news coverage over the last season largely took place *before* Heysel: Kevin Whitton's trial and the police search for the notorious 'Fat Man' involved soccer-related offences from the 1984–5 season. As a result even the better soccer journalists have succumbed to the temptation to believe their own propaganda. For instance, David Lacey of the *Guardian* wrote recently:

> All in all it has been a good season with events on the field providing just the fillip that was needed after tragedies of Bradford and Brussels and the outbreaks of spectator violence that cast gloom over the English game for much of last year . . . There is, of course, no need for complacency. The change in the League's voting structure gives the big clubs more power to shape the competition to their liking and they will surely readdress their minds to this before long. Annual attendances are down by more than a million which means that the figure has slid from 24.6 million to around 16.4 million since 1980. The World Cup may reveal English football's lack of real quality. But at least this time it is possible to end the season talking about soccer statistics rather than casualty figures.

The 1985–6 soccer season has indeed *appeared* to be relatively trouble free. But there is no hard evidence whatsoever to suggest that the government's 'emergency' measures – introduced in the wake of the Bradford City fire disaster, the death of a Leeds United fan at St Andrews, Birmingham and the Heysel débâcle itself – have succeeded in curbing soccer hooliganism, 1980s style. Reliance on police arrest figures at soccer matches, which have been prominent in news bulletins this season, is dangerous ground: to claim that arrests are down is a misleading statistical basis for an analysis of cause and effect (figures for ejections from stadiums are often more reliable signs of trouble matches) and, if anything, merely serves to confirm the acceleration of a tendency over the last decade to locate the site of soccer violence away from the terraces.

'Known' pubs or the seating areas of soccer grounds are current favourites. The publicity given to the 'General' Muranyi case highlighted dominant patterns of soccer's style wars: military-type manoeuvres, ambushes, designer clothes. One incident which did reach the status of national news this year was the aerosol attack – starting to rival the ubiquitous Stanley knife sortie – on Manchester United's players as they left the team coach to play Liverpool at Anfield. Coming as it did shortly after the return of soccer to 'live' TV after months of dispute, there was controversy about how much media attention should be given to it. Kenny Dalglish, Liverpool's player-manager, was quoted as saying that he didn't think that the item should be blown up out of all proportion, but others – notably United officials – were more vitriolic, and sure enough there was considerable coverage on the evening news and in the next morning's papers. What did not hit the headlines, though *The Times* did report it, was the attack on a Manchester fan sitting in the stands during the match itself, which involved several 'well-dressed young men in their twenties' who calmly got up from their seats, viciously set about the 'enemy' and equally calmly sat down again, all without police intervention. Real, *Clockwork Orange*-style mayhem.

Unusually – since abstinence is fast becoming fashionable among top boys – this trouble was put down, partly, to drink. The government's 'quickie' panic law, the Sporting Events (Control of Alcohol etc.) Act 1985, passed without opposition at the height of the post-Heysel hysteria, has been held to be so successful that amendments are to be introduced to relax the ban on alcohol in executive and directors' boxes; 'more booze to the toffs', as Eldon Griffiths, parliamentary spokesman for the Police Federation, put it. But at the same time, changes to the Public Order Bill will make it illegal to consume alcohol in buses or cars carrying more than two people on their way to soccer matches. Since many fans travel by minibus or private car precisely to evade the ever-increasing surveillance of trains and coaches, there are likely to be hostile confrontations as police try to enforce the provision. When this is coupled with other parts of the new legislation, especially the introduction of the catch-all offence of 'disorderly conduct', the civil liberties of ordinary soccer fans will be severely curtailed. Further, the measures are woefully ill-conceived as a 'battle' plan. As one fan boasted to *The Times*: 'The government might stop a repeat of Brussels but they won't stop the fighting outside the grounds and in the cities'.

What can be done? It is one thing to blame the Tory government for its orchestrated panic over hooliganism at soccer matches and for reversal when the going got tough and it became convenient to look in the other direction – similar criticism could, after all, be made about the government's law and order strategy generally. But Labour presided over the nation's development of 'modern' soccer hooliganism in the 1960s. It then responded to the 1970s variety by, under Dennis Howell, caging in the terrace fans with such militaristic precision that the scene was well set for today's self-styled 'barmy armies' to prove their manhood further and further from soccer stadiums, where at least containment was a realistic aim. Labour needs urgently to develop a more coherent and popular leisure policy as well as its own response to crime in the cities. It needs to rid itself of debilitating myths about the 'glorious' past of the 'people's game' and the nation's exploits on the international stage.

Professional soccer in Britain in the 1980s is an entrepreneur's paradise, ripe for a quick killing before the industry gurgles down the plughole. It is a prime example of Margaret Thatcher's philosophy in practice, and who can be surprised if the country's male youth catch something of its narrow, mean and brutish spirit, particularly the xenophobia? An overhaul of soccer's governing bodies is long overdue, let alone a regulation of the game's financial set-up – and a more modest assessment of British soccer's place in the world would go a long way towards channelling national pride into more productive endeavours. The Heysel tragedy should not be allowed to slip out of popular memory so easily; the rehabilitation of soccer in England will take more than a single season – and the appointment of a Labour-voting team manager – but it is a task worth undertaking.

6 The New (Soccer) Men

In many ways it is a savage irony that, since the late 1970s, so many young working-class males have chosen soccer as their fashion page. These terrace and, frequently, stand narcissists have gained public notoriety through their 'casual' style being evident in certain hard-core fighting crews who have carried on soccer hooligan traditions established in the first skinhead surge of twenty years ago. Their methods, however, reverse the images and received notions of soccer violence and vandalism: a temperance where there was over-indulgence, a preference to sit down (expensively) rather than stand up (cheaply), a desire to look 'good' rather than 'hard', and a wish to travel privately instead of with official backing. All of this contributes to the various firms' marked ability to avoid detection, even now that, in the last couple of years, media and eventually police attention has been focused on them. But it is more forgotten that such 'style' obsessions involve young soccer fans on a *mass* scale – not simply the coach and train gangs that replaced the boot boys of yesteryear. Writers like Frank Mort have rightly pointed to both the transition of street style into high-street style and the importance for sexual politics of current fashion's opening up of gender identities for men. What needs to be pinned down, though, is the context – historical and cultural – of such shifting categories.

Soccer in Britain, for a century the opiate of the working *man*, is a surprising location for designer menswear and sportswear and their specific connotations of crises in masculinity. Even a supposedly classic *radical* account of the life and times of a League footballer like Eamon Dunphy's *Only A Game?* celebrates the 'hard men' and recalls that, in what it sees as the 'golden age' of the author's playing days, sport 'was good for you, made a man of you'. Dunphy (1987) also remembers that their 'lives were like other men's lives except for the game. We had children, mortgages, cars that didn't start, wives that bitched, overdrafts, and gardens that needed tending.' Professional soccer was, in fact, for Dunphy a haven in an increasingly heartless world: 'In a darkening world where the shadows of violence, political expediency, materialism and junk culture grow even longer, sport as it is practised by its good pros remains a bastion of decency, a place where virtue is rewarded and cheating exposed.'

Unfortunately, for this *Boys Own* outlook, soccer has long ceased to be an unproblematic 'private' sphere where sexual politics can be left at home. The onslaught of the New Right in the field of soccer has exposed the left's ambivalence on questions of mainly male violence around soccer over the last two decades. Other issues of 'law and order', such as racial attacks and violence against women, have justly become *cause célèbres* for the left, provoking an about-turn on 'crime and punishment' since the late 1960s. However, when the problem is 'soccer hooliganism' – where the same ugly spectres of sexism and racism are manifest – there has more often been a willingness to cite 'moral panics' as cause *and* effect. The present campaigns by government to open up the closed soccer worlds through membership cards, travel bans, exclusion orders and the like may well be motivated by re-election fever plus a will to reclaim the 'law and order' ticket for use in a third term, when 'soccer' can be wheeled out as a motif for the regulation of disorder. But a strategic side of intervention *is* being constructed in the process. Even a policeman biting another's ear off in a rugby match figures in judicial reasoning as 'soccer hooliganism' these days. Especially post-Heysel, the political focus on soccer as a social metaphor for 'disorderly conduct' (enshrined in a special offence in the new Public Order Act 1986) has failed to elicit any coherent response from the left.

Part of the left's problem lies in an acceptance of traditional masculine roles and identities which soccer in Britain has come to signify. The decline and fall of the 'people's game' – a male myth if ever there was one – has been littered with calls, from traditionalists as well as Tories, for a return to a 1950s-style mass spectator sport: that is, *before* modernism, when players are said to have become greedy and less differential while hooligans run amok. Traditional or 'real' soccer is associated with all kinds of elements – controlled wages, regionalization in lower divisions, peaceful terraces disciplined by one policeman and his dog – but most of all it represents, precisely, Dunphy's conception of the 'man's game' which he sees as, eventually, having been strangled by modern times. Right from long lost origins in the 1870s, professional soccer in Britain has depended on males, and their sons, for an overwhelming majority of its paying customers. In this sense, 'family enclosures' (so fêted by Margaret Thatcher's regime) are innovative rather than a revival of a lost soccer watching community, though they are highly unlikely to prevent much recurrent violence.

Deeply embedded in this popular mythology is the notion that on the field there is a masculine style of British soccer – hewed initially out of hard labour – which became corrupted by modern influences from the 1950s onwards, with 'continental' role models taking over. Skilful or 'flair' (including all non-white) players have fallen foul of this prejudice – they don't have the 'bottle' in dressing room argot – and it sustains the bias of the Football Association, not to mention the judiciary, when it comes to preventing women playing soccer on the same level as men. The FA secretary, Ted Croker, appeared not so long ago on an Open University programme on 'women and sport' to tell us that women footballers were irrevocably handicapped by the shape of their chests, which men used, in time-honoured fashion, to control the ball. Ah, *those* golden days! Flat caps, rattles, long shorts, centre-partings *and* chest traps; when men were men and went off to the soccer, and women stayed at home to wash the kit. As the BBC's recent documentary *Home and Away* emphasized, British women footballers have to go as far away as Italy to sell their labour power as professionals, though the film felt compelled to reintroduce stereotyped images of 'femininity' by dwelling, longingly, on their consumer habits. Imagine a documentary on, say, Manchester United players following them around with the shopping trolley in Wilmslow!

'Post-punk' soccer style is important only in this context. It represents, both on the field and off, a combination of sharp challenges to traditional conceptions of masculinity (and to modes of soccer watching and playing, too) together with a knowingly cynical, indigenous extension of both traditional and modern soccer violence. The regional style wars, rivalries played out in fashion fads and poses, which have spread outwards from the north-west for nearly a decade now, constitute a postmodern reaction to the absurdities of the modern game. As 'pop' closed its gates to the dole generation and moved in an 'old youth' as a lucrative market, match days took on a whole new meaning.

This was soccer with a *difference*, all right. Of all the sites to choose as a catwalk for Pringle, Chester Barrie or Burberry! Economic strangulation of the regions and an increasing national recognition that, as the style wars have intensified due to all the recent publicity, expensive gear will be ripped and torn have cut the scope for experimentation so that style changes have inevitably slowed. Also as the old 'skin' connection with soccer hooliganism is finally counted out, even by the police and courts, the 'new' style is rapidly becoming the basis for the exercise of discretion in policing, contributing along with the high street to much more standardization in trousers, jackets, jumpers and shoes, though 'smartness' is, as always, still significant in this new and mod sensibility.

As Eugene McLaughlin[1] has pointed out, there is no causal link between youth subcultures, male fashions, sexuality and left politics. But what *is* the political status of the casuals' redrawing of the boundaries of professional soccer's terrain? Well before the images of Luton's invasion by Millwall flickered on to the prime minister's television set in March 1985, the contours of the domain of soccer's masculine world were being renegotiated, bringing, as Frank Mort has indicated, considerable physical danger to some of those who dared to 'deviate'. The rivalries *within* loyal support, at Celtic and elsewhere, are legendary: pink cardigans do not always rule OK! But the left cannot ignore the fact that beneath the far-from-skin-deep body politics of soccer chic the same old atavistic desires persist. Thatcher's reign has witnessed the reassertion of traditional notions of masculinity with some vengeance – in places as far apart as Port Stanley and Brussels – and a left which continues to see in this only either a 'pathological' lower-working-class violence or, worse, the seeds of a proletarian resistance movement is badly off beam. The New Football Man is created by a whole series of discourses – from fashion, sport, politics and so on – but we should be mindful of what the journalist Arthur Hopcraft (1968) wrote about a slightly older version: 'Football crowds are never going to sound or look like the hat parade on the club lawns of Cheltenham racecourse. They are always going to have more vinegar than Chanel.'

7 Shamble On

Who would have thought that the most subversive pop voice of 1986 would be pitched somewhere between the girl group teen pop of the Shangri-Las and the folk purity of Sandy Denny? The Shop Assistants, and lately the Primitives and Talulah Gosh, set a soul-less, pre-adolescent female vocal against either raucous Ramones post-punk noise or else gentle, almost shy, jangly guitar. This innocence is highly contrived, of course, and perfectly matches 'shambling' bands – an epithet by John Peel, out of shambolic and rambling, stylized lack of experience and musical (in)competence. What is perhaps even more calculating is the coy referencing of pop and youth culture, history. This is a key feature of shambling's sound: in particular, 1960s folk rock and 1970s punk.

The contradictions between these two golden 'moments' of cultural politics are played out in the music's textures: 1968 versus 1976, hippie versus punk, feedback versus three-chord thrash, authenticity versus artifice. What is interesting is that, ten years on from punk and in the wake of stern proclamations about the end of 'youth culture', a heyday of 'rockville' – a faith in the music's *innate* ability to 'set us free' – is apparently being returned to. It's almost as if punk had never happened, as Dave Rimmer (1985) put it in his history of the 'new pop' and Culture Club. Guitar bands, protest singers, hippy convoys stalk the land like there *was* no Sid Vicious, and a white music scene now dominates the 'indie' charts, mixing mannered nostalgia for the myths of the 1960s with various musical forms (folk, country, psychedelia, rockabilly, garage) which are plundered for their 'rootsiness'. In all the rush to define what punk meant – socially, musically, culturally, politically – there has been little explanation of why the most pertinent influences in the new bohemia are the likes of Captain Beefheart, at one extreme, and Bob Dylan, at the other.

One clue lies in the fact that it is 'rock' itself which is now deemed to have 'roots', located in various different (take your pick!) periods in the 1960s before the disillusionment set in. Rock's dream, amalgamating counter-culture with a certain musical style, fossilizing it politically in the process, is far from over. Whether we agree with the music press that it is Bruce Springsteen and the E Street Band, or the Smiths, or whoever, that consti-tute the 'last great rock band' is beside the point. The power of rock lies not simply in its political economy or profits, but in its proven ability to produce and circulate 'meaning', primarily the message of its *own* cultural force – to bind people in 'community', to be 'authentic' and so on. Its success in yoking successive 'rebellious' youth subcultures to specific musical forms – styles of 'nonconformity' apparently endlessly coming round again – is a testament to its pervasive durable effect. Punk is the archetype. Subculture, style and sound: shrink-wrapped for the pop culture archivist. Not the *end* of rock/youth culture nexus, but its most perfect product.

What makes shambling bands refreshing is not that they break musical barriers as such, or that they are an embryonic youth culture in the making. The sounds themselves have all been heard before (though, crucially, not necessarily together at the same time): it's more the way the two decades clash; *both* 'punk' and 'folk' rock, for instance, appear here as conventions, neither more 'real' or expensive of 'true' emotion than the other. The whole 'indie-pop' scene is far too disparate and changeable to be categorised by one label, however nifty, and the media obsession with pigeon-holing (anorak brigade/cuties/sweeties are already doing the rounds) ought to be resisted at all costs. This is, though, easier said than done. Last year's 'underground' heroes are already signed to a major label (Shop Assistants to Chrysalis through Blue Guitar) and the heat is on the 'indie' sector to produce the Next Big Thing as in the 1970s with punk.

Whatever else happens in 1987, this likely election year is bound to witness an intensification of struggle over the 'politics of youth culture' as the parties strain to read the pop signposts to the youth vote. 'Style' and its metamorphosis into the 'new authenticity' are highly misleading notions if taken at face value; deeply dangerous terrain for those seeking a rebellious youth culture, a 'new punk'. The new pop may have had its day, and a more socially conscious phase (lyrics, rhetoric, even political affiliation) replayed in post-Live Aid, but it all remains part of the merry-go-round. Shambling bands represent more than a timely desire to refuse political citizenship, to fail to 'grow up': they are a bright, disruptive influence on rock's power plays and consequently might – just might – sow some seeds for a more optimistic future.

Discography

Shop Assistants, *Shop Assistants* (Blue Guitar)
Shop Assistants, *Safety Net* (53rd and 3rd)
Shop Assistants, *All Day Long* (Subway)
Talulah Gosh, *Steaming Train* (53rd and 3rd)
Talulah Gosh, *Beatnik Boy* (53rd and 3rd)

8 What's so Funny 'Bout Peace, Love and Understanding?

'What matters now is not the rise and fall of punk but why the Shop Assistants sound like Judy Collins'. So noted music critic Simon Frith in the *Observer* on 16 March 1986. At long last it seems we may have entered the era of post-post-punk. Not that the past is gone, though. Like the poor, it seems, it is always with us, however hard we try to wriggle free. Certain strands of popular culture in the late 1980s recall high points in the cultural politics of the last two decades. Those peaks symbolized by 1968 and 1976, the counter-cultures of the 'hippies' and 'punks', are being scaled again for quite different purposes and in an entirely different context, giving rise to possible new evaluation of received wisdoms. Hence, popular cultural forms, especially musical forms like folk, punk, protest, psychedelia and country are being ripped out of their original, 'authentic' setting by a *new* white bohemia in order to build and sustain a new kind of counter-culture in a much more hostile political, economic and social climate.

It seems as if Dave Rimmer had it pinned down when he described the story of 'new pop' heroes Culture Club and Boy George with the epitaph *Like Punk Never Happened* (Rimmer 1985). Guitar bands, protest singers, festivals and wandering 'hippies' are all the key aspects of pop culture in 1987 – even though the charts reflect few of such 1960s phenomena explicitly today. Artists whose reputation was made in that era, such as Bob Dylan, are curiously the unspoken inspirations for the young post-punk generation of the new recession, rather than, for instance, the Sex Pistols. While Dylan himself continues to, for the most part, churn out turgid, reactionary material (though his reinterpretation of old 1960s songs continues to surprise the critics as well as his younger audiences who are hearing them for the first time), self-styled 'Jewish, lesbian folksingers' (Phranc) rifle his back catalogue to produce contemporary reworkings of 'The lonesome death of Hattie Carroll' and Suzanne Vega emerges from the New York coffee-house scene like it was 1963 again. Organ, bass, drums, guitar line-ups are drawn increasingly, inevitably it seems, to where Dylan left off in the mid-1960s with *Highway 61 revisited* and *Blonde on blonde*.

Long-time folk heroes like the former Fairport Convention guitarist, Richard Thompson, are finally getting heard and appreciated by a much wider audience (particularly in the USA), and find themselves on the same bill as unruly 'punk folkies' such as the Pogues, as well as the role models for the young vanguard of musicians who, in the past, cringed at the adult-oriented rock (AOR) output of these 'golden oldies'. Peter Buck, guitarist with Georgia's REM, insists: 'I've been listening to Richard Thompson since I was a kid and he's probably the best songwriter of the last fifteen years . . . He reaches to the heart without being maudlin or excessive. What the hell, he's fuckin' great.' Johnny Marr, guitarist with Manchester's Smiths remembers: 'When I was able to start putting chords together I was turned on to Bert Jansch, Pentangle and Richard Thompson and, because of him, to Jerry Donahue.'

On the face of it, punk's explosion over a decade ago might have put paid to such indebtedness, to heartfelt deference to figures associated with a 'discredited' past, but nothing could be further from the truth. Among punk's myriad meanings, the myth of its role as the hippies' revenge, extinguishing the 'peace and love' logo in the process, is the least understood. In the wake of postmodern times, MTV, the 'new pop', the recycling of 'authenticity', the death of the soul boy craving on the one hand and the rise of a new 'less than zero' blank generation (think of writers like Bret Easton Ellis) on the other, has left a space of experiments with the accepted conventions associated with 'hippie' and 'punk'. Playing with the musical and political signs of the past formations has become a new obsession for the 'dispossessed' young 1980s generation, locked out of Style's house of fun. As Jon Savage has put it:

> In the space torn between styles, what interests me is not a return to rock – in America it never went away . . . but the chance that there is for the voices that have been excluded by Style Culture's metropolitan bias to make themselves heard. There is a new, uncharted area of youth culture: it might include the Rock fans or Goths that populate any provincial city or small town . . . it will also include another group which because it is not organised in consumption, is not deemed worthy of media attention. These days, this means that it might as well not exist. Yet any observer will have noted a large amount of people disparagingly called 'hippies' who operate like the *Wandervögel* of the Twenties, moving from town to town, from festival to 'Peace Convoy', outside the bounds of normal society. Any future account of pop culture must include their bohemian wanderings which are a true index of consumerism in crisis.

Songs of Innocence and Experience

As the 'casuals' on soccer terraces in the 1980s can be regarded as a caricature of the new yuppie affluence and an ironic, postmodernist joke at the
expense of those who laughed loud at the decaying fabric of the inner cities,
the new bohemia is not simply a hippie revival. As Simon Reynolds[1] has
made clear, this predominantly white backlash to the 'health'[2] of chart pop
is united by the deepest suspicion of certain, taken-for-granted 'hippie'
values. Reynolds has also argued:

> The 'shambling bands' have widely diverging influences – ranging from Sixties
> garage and psychedelia to the Velvet Underground to the thrash-pop of The
> Buzzcocks and Ramones to spikey indie-pop circa 1979. But there *is* a
> common legacy derived from punk – a hatred of anything hippy (long tracks,
> virtuosity, complex instrumentation, mysticism, pomp, fusion). This anti-
> hippie consensus has itself settled over the decade, ossifying into stifling
> orthodoxy – an insistence on short songs, lo-fi, minimalism, purism and
> guitars, guitars, guitars.

'Shambling' pop (from the Smiths through the Shop Assistants to the Pastels),
with its emphasis on the 1960s, childhood innocence and a refusal to grow
up, is one example of the new bohemia in the 1980s. As Reynolds has also
commented in a stark comparison of white rock with black pop: 'White
bohemian rock is downwardly aspiring, looking to the past for "roots", for
the lost "real" of suffering. Black pop takes conventional upward aspirations,
conventional sexual protocol, and turns them into a cartoon utopia. There's
a vast chasm between white rock and black pop . . .'.

There is no easy return to 'rockville' here: to when rock was young and
had no roots of its own and when a counter-culture could place its faith in
the capacity of rock music to set us free. The states of 'innocence' and
'experience' that 'shambling' pop alludes to are highly contrived and cannot
be simply read off with the aid of a musical semiotics. Postmodern
knowingness allied to a keen sense of pop history enable this new 'new wave'
– whether more conventionally based on 1960s pop or more left field
experimental[3] – to avoid easy categorization, media pigeon-holing and the
desires of pop sociologists for a new 'punk' youth culture. In this sense, there
is a sharp contrast between the mannered refusal to 'grow up' of the
'shambling' bands, a state of mind which is frequently evident in their dress
sense[4] and choice of names (Mighty Lemon Drops, Woodentops, Talulah
Gosh and so on), and the world-weary cynicism of the experienced, more
'professional', older bands who have turned to 1960s musical forms for their
'roots'.

Musically, the best example of this is Edinburgh's Shop Assistants,[5] whose initial releases were put on the small independent label '53rd and 3rd', but who 'graduated' to a major for their eponymous debut LP. Their vocal style – pre-pubescent girl voice against Ramones noise or jangling Byrds guitar – very deliberately pits child-like female purity with 'post-feminist' lyrics. On 'I don't wanna be friends with you', lead vocalist Alex sings, as Simon Frith noted, in a style recalling folk-rock female songstresses Judy Collins and Sandy Denny. At high speed:

> You loved me and now you wanna leave me
> Think too much of me to deceive me
> Say you wanna go while we're still friends
> But I believe in the bitter end
> If you don't love me anymore
> Just tell me you don't want to know
> But I don't wanna be civilised
> You leave me and I'll scratch your eyes out
> I don't wanna be friends with you
> I will never be friends with you.

What is most interesting about the Shop Assistants and their ilk is the search and struggle for new (folk) anti-rock conventions, which helps their music to express and construct the contradictory emotions of the modern world: loss, nostalgia, despair and solidarity as well as 'innocence' and 'experience'. What 'shambling' shares with the most progressive of other genres in popular music is the important sense of the West's desolation, and a desire for a return not to a simplistic optimism of the will (in politics, youth culture, 'post-industrial' society), but to a mythology of 'innocence' *before* hope was trampled. The exact location of this rainbow's end is, of course, uncertain. But it connects inextricably with the popular memory of the 1960s. This memory is itself constructed. As Robert Shelton, author of a Bob Dylan biography (Shelton, 1986), has noted:

> The worst thing about the sixties is not what happened then, but what has happened since it ended. The sixties is not contained in 1960 to 1969. The sixties were really in two decades: it began in '55 and ended in '74. It began with all the incredible recording activity – Chuck Berry's 'Maybelline' and all the folks that were being recorded by the early rock people. It ended with the evacuation of Saigon. That's what I call the sixties – twenty years.

Shelton's account of Dylan spans a similar period, tailing off markedly after the singer's 'Tangled up in blue' period. Writing about Britain, Robert Hewison in his book *Too Much* (Hewison, 1986) argues:

The Sixties were good at a number of things, especially at having a good time, and now, when we are having a bad time, we are inclined to read the words 'too much' with a guilty awareness that the rich substances of the Sixties has been dissipated in the Eighties and that it was in the Seventies that we began to pay the price.

Of course, it is much more complicated than that, and at this distance from events there is still confusion about what took place, as well as ambivalence about its significance. This is because people in the Sixties were particularly prone to mixing myth and reality, style and substance, image and fact. The Sixties have themselves passed into myth more quickly than the period that preceded them.

Peter York, the style counsellor approvingly quoted by Hewison, wrote at the end of the 1970s for *Harpers and Queen*:

> What is certain is that eye-witness accounts differ radically, not only as to what mattered in the sixties, but about what actually happened. But when asked about the sixties there seems to be a qualitative difference in people's responses – they seem to be confused about what really happened (to them) and what the media had said was happening. This kind of conceptualising seems true across the social board. Most people under forty, in describing the sixties, at least defer to the media sixties.
>
> My own main sixties memories, however, seem to be about *things* – having them and wanting them . . . The reality of the sixties was new money, new technology, *things* – and the choices they implied.

For a post-punk generation of 'indie-pop' bands, most of whom were not born in the 1960s, there is a veritable *mélange* of 'memories' – musical and cultural – to draw on, recycle and discard. Rock naivety, though, is *not* an option. 'Hippies' in this new, meta-language means 'experience' of the 1960s, and its rock myths, first hand. As Wayne Hussey, lead singer of successful goth band The Mission (whose music directly recalls the late 1960s and early 1970s, reflected in their long-haired fashions and Hendrix, Neil Young and Led Zeppelin infatuations) has argued forcefully: 'A lot of people say we're hippies. Well, we're not, we're punks.'

It is only in this context that the 'folk' or 'folk-rock' revival of the mid-1980s can be properly understood. In England, at least, there seems to be a wave of enthusiasm (audience, critics, music industry) once again for 'folk' forms. This has already happened on at least two occasions this century, so cynics may justifiably question the labelling of another rock culture fad as a 'revival'; but there are significant features of the move *back* to folk, away from rock, which may be of more lasting value in cultural politics than yesterday's model. As *Folk Roots* editor, folk and blues musician Ian A. Anderson has pointed out: 'younger artists and groups (and quite a few not so young ones) in Britain and elsewhere are increasingly turning to *roots* influences from home and abroad on the less trivial fringes of commercial music'.

This new 'folk–rock' sensibility *is* different to its predecessors. It is wide ranging, encompassing as it does the Shop Assistants' post-punk 'cutie'[6] sexual politics, the ethnic 'folk' of various countries of Africa as well as the protest songs of Dick Gaughan and Christy Moore. It differs from the 'pre-feminist' 1960s in its opening up of the 'private' sphere where the personal is political, and yet it finds 'traditional' solidarity in mining and other communities engaged in industrial struggles against pit and works closure just as 'folk' has always done. The clash of such ideologies, where women are at once domesticated *and* resisting domesticity, is forcing male musicians to come to terms with the limits of folk forms and conventions.

Billy Bragg, for example, released an EP *Between the Wars* during the British miners' strike of 1984–5, dedicated to the work of the Miners' Wives Support Groups and including Leon Rosselson's 'World turned upside down' and an adapted version of Florence Reece's 'Which side are you on?' as well as a title track written by Bragg which specifically addressed the audience in celebration of the male manual worker ('miner', 'docker') of yesteryear. The record was commercially very successful in Britain, bringing the 'Barking bard' to a new public, but it stands in stark contrast to his later songs which express doubt about personal relationships as well as the moral values of late capitalism. These songs cross over to a pop style which allows less certainty about the world than the 'protest' songs of working–class solidarity. On his 'Walk away Renee' version (Johnny Marr on guitar picking out the old Four Tops melody), on the chart-busting *Levi Stubbs' Tears* EP, and on the *Talking with the Taxman about Poetry* LP, there is a self-deprecating humour and an openness missing from his earlier punk thrashes. As he wryly admits on 'Greetings to the new brunette' from the 'difficult third album' (again with Marr's aid):

> Shirley,
> your sexual politics have left me all of a muddle
> Shirley,
> we are joined in the ideological cuddle
> I'm celebrating my love for you
> With a pint of beer and a new tattoo . . .
> Politics and pregnancy
> Are debated as we empty our glasses.

This male notion of the 'people' in folk, and the patriarchal values that it enshrines, is undercut both by the calculated joining of punk's three-chord wonderment and a vocal style mixing little girl purity with 1960s 'teen pop' (the Shop Assistants, Talulah Gosh, the Primitives and other 'indie'[7] bands) and by post-punk 'folksingers' like Michelle Shocked and Phranc. Phranc's style – like a female Loudon Wainwright, androgynous enough to make Annie Lennox look feminine – and her 'out' lyrics, and Michelle Shocked's use of pop media to make feminist commitments reflect a quite distinct movement out of the ghetto of 'women's music'. It is not simply feminist questions which are being addressed anew, against the prevailing 'folk' and 'rock' ideologies, by these artists. In any case, punk's most radical effect was its role as culture shock. It raised in particular, beyond the debates about gender and sexuality which much of the new pop explored, the spectre of a bloated music industry which was inexorably committed to pumping every last drop out of consumerism, to commodification of everything (even itself). Further, it fundamentally subverted pop's previous notions of 'authenticity' and 'truthfulness'. Not that punk achieved a 'new' authenticity; it was easily, too easily, incorporated after a few short months and packaged for the youth culture archives. But in both these spheres, the industry and the music, there is a punk legacy for future generations to draw on.

One example of punk's meaning being taken up by the 'new folk' is in the area of production. Against a hi-tech, multi-million dollar industry the recording of an artist like Michelle Shocked on a Sony portable in the middle of a field with only the crickets and passing trucks for company was, at least, a major departure. The success of the LP *The Texas Campfire Tapes*[8] in the British independent charts was only surpassed, in 1986, by the reception given to another guitar/vocal troubadour, ex-convict and long-time Los Angeles busker Ted Hawkins. Both the albums *Watch Your Step* and *On the Boardwalk: the Venice beach tapes*, released again on small, independent labels, were significant not so much for the new sound (Sam Cooke's vocal style twenty years on is, as David Toop commented in his music column in *The Face*, nothing to shout home about in itself) or their originality (*Venice Beach Tapes* contained covers of Sam Cooke, Hank Williams and even John Denver!); they were significant more as a register of a new interest in a supposed accessibility and expression of 'raw' feeling which Hawkins personifies, both on stage and on record. The 'discovery' of Hawkins by British DJ Andy Kershaw (himself responsible, almost single-handedly for the 'roots' music playlists on BBC radio) and his subsequent transplanting to the UK, like a kind of twentieth-century Kaspar Hauser, added to the mythology of his rise to trendy folk idol.

Live performances in themselves have become worthy of note in such unlikely success stories of the video age. 'Folk' as style is less important here than simply somewhere cheap and easy to play. In some senses, all Michelle Shocked and Ted Hawkins have done is carry on their 'busking' and 'festival hopping', but to larger and more sympathetic audiences in Britain. Their music cuts across *various* styles (pop, blues, country); their unity is only in their 'have guitar and voice, will travel' motto. As an English exponent of such one-'man' bandwagoning, Clive Gregson[9] (ex-Any Trouble leader, and member of Richard Thompson's band) put it like this: 'the so-called trend towards folk is more a matter of economics: if there's no money to be made in touring you might as well go out with the fewest possible overheads'.

Gregson confirmed, too, that his sometime band leader, Thompson, is less than enamoured with the folk scene in Britain anyway, and with the old, 'folkie' ideology which has restricted cross-fertilization of different musical traditions. As Thompson has argued:

> The Folk scene needs changing – I'm trying to bring about a revolution . . . it's a matter of organisation, in the sense that Folk clubs are dying on their feet, what you need is to professionalise say 20 folk clubs in Britain. Give them excellent PA systems, good seating, improve the decor, and make it a circuit where you can put on really good people and ensure that they get paid real money. You need to create something in between the standard sized 'Rock' gig and the Folk club, you've got to find a middle stage because too many people get labelled jazz and ignored. What you want is a place where jazz, folk, left of field rock etc. can all be staged in one venue . . . a circuit of clubs.

Certainly the continuities with the 'pub rock' element in punk are plain. The general ethos of both the 'new folk' and the 'old punk' is anti-'stadium rock' and 'megabuck' pop values: however, whether the fresh-faced idealism of the present will go the way of the past attempts to disrupt rock's proven power is another question.

Taken at face value, the formations around the terms 'folk' and 'punk' suggest the antithesis of rock. Folk ideology has always been important in supplementing rock's claim to cultural esteem, but it has constantly provided a means of critique as the rock machine failed to 'turn us on' through the 1970s and 1980s. Punk claimed to have buried rock once and for all. With the collapse of 'rock' and 'pop' distinctions, post-punk critics can (studiously, ironically) 'play' with pop life *as* real life, but the postmodernist black hole beckons around the corner. Revivals of folk-rock and other roots musics cannot avoid being a part of the pop music industry's desperate attempts to pull new rabbits out of old hats alongside 'new age', 'hi-NRG' or whatever. There may well be an urgent need for a 'new music' that would capture and extend an emerging political consciousness; but an acknowledgement that rock is an extremely powerful medium among the youth of the country, perhaps *the* most powerful, is an inadequate response to the rock discourse of the past twenty or thirty years.

The meanings of 'folk' and 'punk', the moments of hippie counter-culture and punk's 'no future', are inextricably bound up with the pop industry's progress, not simply to retain and develop 'market share' and exploit 'new technologies', but to circulate and recirculate new meanings. The diversity of 'folk' meanings, folk as opposed to rock/commerce, folk as opposed to punk/post-punk, is an integral part of that circulation, just as the punk sensibility of 'anyone can play' street credibility was always a myth. None of this should make us any less ready to champion a cultural politics which values music and musicians who can bring a sense of urgency to a counter-cultural movement. As Greil Marcus[10] has pleaded, reviewing versions of the song 'What's so funny 'bout peace, love and understanding?' both by the writer Nick Lowe and later by Elvis Costello: 'What's so funny 'bout peace, love and understanding? Now, nothing. For an instant, the search for peace, love and understanding is what life is all about.' It should, though, make us more wary of rock myths and folk ideologies.

9 The Age of Rock

1987 is just like old times really. A new Fleetwood Mac blockbuster zooming up the album charts, Johnny Walker on the radio and a cluster of ageing rock stars collected together on an LP, having strutted their stuff and rattled their jewellery for royalty and a large hand-clapping audience live and on television. The sheer *health* of the rock industry is what comes over these days: in the quality of production on vinyl (or, more significantly, compact disc), the vitality of movement on stage or video (think of Tina Turner) and the super-efficiency of the playing. What could possibly be wrong with these values? Value *for* money, a consumer paradise where darkness, uncertainty and doubt have no place, the ultimate rock wet dream. No danger. Naughty but nice, safe as sex.

One reason for the continuing success of these AOR products (which Phil Collins and Genesis epitomize so well – even when they protest that it's all done in the best possible taste, complete with Spitting Imagery) is simply age. Rock's audience (like so many of its performers) is getting older and, like pre-rock generations, is largely sinking into complacent affluence the further it gets from its youth. The career of an artist such as Eric Clapton is an excellent illustration of the stages of this process. Looking back from the 'rock dinosaur' award at this year's nauseating BPI extravaganza, 'Slowhand' (no irony any more) surveys a quarter of a century in showbiz: from blues fiend to guitar deity in a few short years in the 1960s, followed by heroin addiction and a few ill-chosen Powellite sentiments – which helped to fuel the Rock Against Racism fire – only for pop media rehabilitation to snare him in the 1980s. Clapton has been quoted as saying that a performer *inevitably* loses something that motivates him or her at the age of around 40. Maybe it's just that, as Steve Turner's book *Conversations with Eric Clapton* (1976), hinted, he didn't have that much to say anyway. At a time when the tabloids are hunting down younger hard drug users like Boy George, and exposing fellow Prince's Trust star Elton John, to be so uncontroversial must be something of a relief, a lifestyle to go with the bland-out of the music. The score for BBC television's nucleur thriller *Edge of Darkness*, though, was a marked departure: much preferable to the album track used for Martin Scorsese's *The Color of Money*. Like Mark Knopfler's film work on *Cal* and *Local Hero*, there's a sensitivity here to prove that there may be life in Chuck Berry's monsters of rock after all.

But age is not simply a biological or psychological category in AOR. If rock can construct, so efficiently and pervasively, alongside other media, a 'youth' market over a thirty-year time span, it can certainly be relied on to sustain an 'adult' constituency. The decline of the single, the predominance of the over-30s in the media industries, the conscious targeting of the over-25 (mainly male) audience of potential Q readers and the high-speed development of new technologies to displace battered album collections are all well advanced. What is more subtle is the recycling of the 1970s that is at work somewhere in all this: it is, naturally, a partisan notion of that decade (shorn of punk, ignorant of glam), but it carries a powerful message: that rock can make you *feel* young. Too old to die (in rock terms), too old to rock'n'roll? Don't worry: Dave Lee Travis is still on the radio to prove you wrong. There is a voice which puts this better than any words I can think of, and it is Paul Simon's. Forget the ANC controversy surrounding his recording in South Africa – incontrovertibly breaking the boycott of South Africa – and the equally unarguably riveting contributions of the musicians on *Graceland*. The sound of what Simon says – however sincere the sentiment – is just pure rock muzack. He comes across as no older, no wiser than when he first sang 'The sound of silence'.

For all their similarity, over-emphasized production values, slick style and 1970s roots, I'd rather listen to Anita Baker or Luther Vandross any day. At least *their* voices don't sound tired, complacent, naive or clapped out. If the vision of the future has to include compact-disc, technical-purity AOR everywhere from the supermarket checkout to the tube station, let it be these desiring vocals that emanate from the speakers.

Discography

Paul Simon, *Graceland* (Warner Bros)
Eric Clapton, *August* (Duck)
Dire Straits, *Brothers in Arms* (Phonogram)
Fleetwood Mac, *Tango in the Night* (Warner Bros)

Genesis, *Invisible Touch* (Virgin)
Luther Vandross, *Give Me the Reason* (Epic)
Tina Turner, *Break Every Rule* (Capitol)
Anita Baker, *Rapture* (Elektra)

10 Down the Tube: Pop on Television

Every time you turn the television on in 1987, Muriel Gray seems to be there. *Frocks on the Box*, trailers for *The Media Show*, you name it. One floor spot she doesn't occupy any more, though, is *The Tube* – she got out just in time, before the plug was pulled. Her co-presenters, Jools and Paula, have stayed on to the bitter end. Reaping the ignominy of the bottomless depths of 'alternative' comedy (Holland's part in the Christmas débâcle on Channel 4, which has led to so many games of musical chairs at Tyne Tees) and the long demise of the 'new pop' phase (in retrospect it was Yates' husband's Live Aid which formed its epitaph), *The Tube* has finally been axed. Just when no one cared enough any more, after a five-year stint as the 1980s *Ready Steady Go*, the 'style' of the show signed its own death warrant.

But before everybody stifles a yawn, it's worth considering the next moves in broadcasting. The moral and political backlash which has helped to finish off *The Tube* is as important as the programme's lost musical and cultural direction. The onslaught on public service TV – which is much more than simply Mary Whitehouse and Norman Tebbit's interventions – will be followed by deregulation and a flurry of new technologies (video, cable, satellite, etc.) which pose both possibilities and pitfalls for pop on television. There *will* be opportunities to break out of the stranglehold of 'megabuck rock', but pop's reputation as the commodity most famous for selling itself will surely be enhanced. In truth, it is pop (not Muriel Gray) that pervades our television screens (selling, promoting, hustling, celebrating, commiserating, titillating), but it is a pop that is ever more carefully controlled. With *Whistle Test* – even less loved than *The Tube* – on the way out, too, it is hard to resist the idea that an era is over. Meanwhile, fast forward the pop-saturated adverts and thrill to John Byrne/Robbie Coltrane/Emma Thompson's *Tutti Frutti* and a *real* pastiche of *Ready Steady Go*; better than *The Tube* could ever manage.

11 Post-pop

1987 may not *seem* much different from 1983: mass unemployment, disintegrating public services, ravaged inner cities and long leads for the Tories in the opinion polls. A rabidly conservative music industry still gorges itself on the last of the big spenders (the post-war baby boomers) and the tabloids throw up any old story that links pop, lust and addiction together. The 1980s version of sex, drugs and rock'n'roll is a particularly nasty tale far removed from the 1960s counter-culture that spawned the idea in the first place. But for once in the history of pop, the middle of a decade has *not* produced an upheaval: the 1950s, 1960s and 1970s all witnessed spectacular cultural formations which might have led us to predict new eruptions in this lineage between the elections of 1983 and 1987. They didn't happen and, moreover, we may have to get used to the view that there will be no repetition of them in the future. In that sense, these are quite significant times for the politics of pop: post-pop politics in fact.

One of the most obvious fashions to enter the pop market place in the four more years since June 1983 is, ironically, protest. 'New popsters' galore have queued up to jump on the 'social conscience' bandwagon set rolling by Band Aid – Gary Kemp of Spandau Ballet for Red Wedge, Duran Duran for Amnesty International – and the musical form itself (guitar, vocal, concerned lyrics) has experienced something of a revival. Radio 1 saw fit recently to broadcast a documentary history (*Rebel Yell*, commentary by John Peel) which emphasized the solid traditions of protest, rooted in folk sensibilities. But earnestness, and putting your mouth where your money is, are no longer enough – if they ever were.

At the 1987 Glastonbury – whether it is a wake (as seems more likely) for a Britain under a re-elected Thatcher government, or a muted celebration

– the diversity of pop's link to dissent and nonconformity is on show. From 'indie-pop' through 'new jazz' to the Manc 'thrust pop' of New Order and the 'barrio roots' of Los Lobos, the range of musical styles is healthily wide: a testament to the myriad counter-cultures which Thatcher/Reagan politics have helped to create. The two most intriguing acts, though, remain the straightforward folk/punk protest of The Men They Couldn't Hang, whose rebel-rousing chorus songs like 'The ghosts of Cable Street' have rightly become renowned, and the more oblique post-punk venom of Elvis Costello.

It's hard to believe that Declan McManus has been punching the pop clock for a decade now (almost as long as the Tories have been in office), but his sneering voice – it's not simply what he says but the way he *slurs* it – stands as *the* sound of pop protest in the Thatcher years. Resentful, bitter, damaged. Sure 'Shipbuilding' and 'Peace in our time' – more conventionally protest songs in lyric and style – are well remembered, but 1986's 'Tokyo storm warning' and 'I want you' (singles from the *Blood and Chocolate* album recorded, once again, with the Attractions) are chilling in their political and personal desolation. It was Costello, after all, who provided the savage irony at Live Aid with his rendition (electric guitar, vocal) of that old northern folk song 'All you need is love', while all around him 'protested' at African famine through a haze of western affluence. Wembley/Philadelphia 'nation' looked pretty much like an earlier incarnation in another decade with the same false dreams. What will he make of *glasnost* and Glastonbury in 1987? Book now to avoid disappointment.

12 Pop Time, Acid House

The Summer of 1988: Moral Panic and Acid House

The 'summer of love 1988', itself a reworking of another mythical summer – the summer of love 1967 – looks set to take its place in the hallowed halls of pop legends. While the 1960s once slipped lazily into the early 1970s, pop time has now accelerated with a vengeance – as if reclaiming borrowed time – according the public phenomenon of acid house little more than a long weekend. Or, as the magazine *i-D* would have it, 'three weeks and two days'. This is, more than ever, flash-in-the-pan pop, truly the era of overnight sensations. An elegy begins for a *lost* rather than last summer, because in so many ways it never really happened. A fictional summer is mourned. A lament is played for the unrealized moments, for those missed opportunities. Whoever said nostalgia's not what is used to be?

The pop chroniclers of acid house spent the autumn of 1988 investigating an allegory, unravelling its various, diverse strands. Revealing the stolen signifiers, a 'style with no substance' was exposed, and once again the circular time scales, increasingly identified as 'postmodern', were invoked. 'If they had been born 10 years earlier they would have been punk rockers . . . 20 years taken LSD and listened to Jim Morrison', suggested the *Sunday Times*. The tale was that acid house was nothing new; it was merely another link in the youth subcultural chain, replaying and reworking the 1960s or 1970s. But acid house is *not* a new subculture in this sense; nor is it the long-desired 'new punk' of the late 1980s.

As the appropriations of acid house were traced, a catalogue of plunderings was compiled, an enticing shopping list for the intended acid houser: psychedelia, acid, smiley, beachwear, Lucozade, fluorescent paraphernalia and so on. This was the logic of consumerism writ large – a mainly middle-class, Dionysian culture, abandoning (that is, spending) and offering the 'self' to the market. The music itself – contrary to the *Observer*'s characterisation of it as a 'type of rock music' – fuses two forms, both based on sampling. Acid house, a derivative of Chicago house music dance styles, arrived in the UK with the landmark of Phuture's 'Acid trax', only to mingle with 'Balearic beat', a crazy mixture of Euro-pop, previously exclusive to an Ibizan jet set, which pilfered from Peter Gabriel, New Order and Mandy Smith among others. The sound of acid house was hailed as the acme of reconstitution.

The summer of 1988 was over when, on 1 October, the *Sun* signalled the dawn of acid house as 'cool and groovy'. Then, just as swiftly, the paper took an about-turn and captained an offensive of 'panic' proportions.

'EVIL OF ECSTASY' (*Sun*, 19 October)

'BAN THIS KILLER MUSIC' (*Post*, 24 October)

'ACID HOUSE HORROR' (*Sun*, 25 October)

'DRUG CRAZED ACID HOUSE FANS' (*Sun*, 28 October)

'GIRL 21 DROPS DEAD AT ACID DISCO' (*Sun*, 31 October)

'ACID KIDS LURED TO HOLLAND' (*Daily Mirror*, 14 November)

A chorus of celebrities was called to comment on the state of the nation's youth. Jonathan King preferred to 'call it rubeeesh'. Peter Powell, a Radio 1 DJ, thought it 'the closest thing to mass zombiedom'. Matt Goss, from teen stars Bros, told of his mate who had been to an acid house club, where everybody was 'out of their heads', and 'sensible Rick' Astley astutely noted that 'they may as well call it heroin house'!

Indeed, the media account they refer to was one of 'chilling' dimensions: a tabloid version of the bogeyman, steeped in the familiar language of the horror story. Acid Pied Pipers, the 'Mister Bigs' of acid house – unscrupulous drug-dealers and warehouse party organizers – were witnessed in a seduction of the innocent. Magical bogeymen tempted their unsuspecting prey with their evil wares: ecstasy, acid, 'killer music' that cast its alluring spell. Smiley, here, became a 'sinister calling card' with hypnotic properties, as the unfortunate were sucked into the 'hellish nightmare'.

The real victims in this tale of an evil cult, which the tabloids recounted, promptly materialized, as the generalities of 'youths', 'teenagers' and 'schoolchildren' gave way to specifically gendered subjects. The *Sun* told how '14-year-old Jenny' swallowed ecstasy for the first time. The *Daily Mirror* explained the way in which a 'young girl rolled a joint of cannabis' and how 'three young girls were spotted taking the mind blowing drug LSD', and quoted one 17-year-old girl claiming 'I had some acid on me'.

This portrayal of the typical acid house victim as a 'young woman' culminated in the *Sun* headline 'Acid fiends spike page 3 girl's drink'. It was reported how Spanish men who were spiking girls' drinks 'would lie in wait and rape them'. Here, the greater danger of sexual violation – only previously implied in the talk of sex orgies, outrageous romps and the use of the 'sex drug' ecstasy at acid house parties – is made explicit. Women are thus established as the victims of deviance within the acid house scene.

In the development of this narrative, women were becoming the targets of a double threat, not only of the physical perils of acid itself, but ultimately of the danger of sexual abuse. As *Sun* page 3 girl Tracy Kirby reported, 'apart from the rape attempt, the worst thing was hallucinating about those ants'. Given the jeopardy that the evil of acid house presents to women, they are, ironically, constructed as figures of deviance within it, transgressive in a cult whose only 'legitimate' victims are male – like Gary Haisman, the DJ from D-Mob, who, the *Daily Mirror* reported, found that his chart success with 'We call it acieed' rebounded on him when the tabloid connection of drugs and acid house led to the cancellation of bookings all over the country.

The Return of Youth as Folk Devil

The features of the public face of acid house – white, male, middle class – match those of another media-introduced figure of the summer of 1988, the 'lager lout'. Ministerial rhetoric, especially that of John Patten and Douglas Hurd, emphasized the rural dimensions of the young male with too much money to spend and too much lager inside him, who threatened formerly 'peaceful' country towns and villages. In June, the mass media focused on an Association of Chief Police Officers (ACPO) report that more than 2,000 people were arrested in more than 250 serious public order disturbances between 1987 and 1988, mainly located in the Home Counties. The heartlands of these 'rural riots' were the Thames Valley, Hampshire, Surrey and Suffolk, typically Tory strongholds. The reason for the attention given to the report in early summer was the spate of newly reported disorders in Crowborough, Newbury, Godalming, Andover and other rural places. One police chief inspector, John Hoyle of Dorking Police, was quoted as saying:

> Most of those arrested have been local people, aged between 18 and 25. They seem to have plenty of money to spend and in most cases they have been drinking . . . There were flash points before. In the 1960s it was mods and rockers, in cafés. Now it's in the pubs.

Government ministers such as Douglas Hurd and John Patten – as Margaret Thatcher and Norman Tebbit had done previously throughout the 1980s – invoked the 1960s legacy of 'permissiveness' to rationalize this apparently difficult political problem of law and order. After nine years of Tory rule, and the phenomenon of the new Conservative and conformist youth culminating in the pervasive 'yuppie' spirit, the rural riots and lager louts presented a dreadful spectre of the re-emergence of deviant subcultures. For a government riding high after a third successive general election victory, this might have seemed to be a political stumbling block. Yet the apparent dilemma – for Tory ministers – of the 'well-heeled hooligan' brought with it a scapegoat which could be turned to their own advantage. As long as the stress could be placed on 'middle-class', 'affluent' youth whose violence was caused by alcohol abuse, the 'left' argument that social conditions lead to crime would be nullified. Furthermore, this justified the already accelerating return to 'law and order', elsewhere prompted by the 'new wave' of football violence at Wembley (England versus Scotland) and Stamford Bridge (Chelsea versus Middlesbrough) in May, with the European Championships looming in June.

The summer of acid house marked a space in which this gallery of rogues could congregate. For instance, consider the *News of the World* story (20 October) which had an archetypal 1960s figure, the notorious acid casualty Syd Barrett, ushered in as the lead role in a classic parable of middle-class demise. This moral tale traced the fall of 'Tragic Syd' from 'Pink Floyd rock legend' to a 'pathetic, crazed zombie . . . howling like a dog'. Others who auditioned for the part in this unfolding drama included 'organised gangs of football hooligans such as West Ham's "Inter City Firm"', whom *The Illustrated London News* (October issue) linked to the ecstasy market.

Media publicity on acid house refocused attention on the city, but only the outskirts, the margins of the urban environment, not the inner city which Margaret Thatcher has targeted as ripe for political conquest through policies of 'regeneration'. This was the sound of the suburbs. Warehouses, which have been extensively, and illegally, used for acid house (and other) gatherings, symbolize the problems of space in the post-industrial city. Football grounds, shopping centres, tube and railway stations are, increasingly, put under intense surveillance. Empty warehouses, artefacts from the industrial past (*before* Thatcher) of cities such as Liverpool, Manchester, Sheffield, Bradford and Leeds, are the last refuge of youth in search of a 'good time'. Police raids are making even these spaces vulnerable to a global neighbourhood watch; as Chief Inspector David Hannas of Hampshire Police said after one acid party raid: 'We would ask all responsible people to contact the police if they become aware of these parties, some of which have resulted in tragic consequences.'

Of all the new signs which the 'summer of 1988' posted via the acid house story, the 'trance dance' best registered potential shifts in the ground previously occupied by subcultures. If, after punk, disco represented a return to the 'male gaze', and more traditional notions of sexual relations, acid house offered something of a departure. In a dance which 'requires no expertise whatsoever', there is a fracturing of the 'male gaze', which has commonly structured the body in dance in pop history. Instead of, as usual, the female body being subjected to the ever-present 'look', the dancers (not just on the dancefloor, but everywhere in range of the beat) turn in on themselves, impeding the meanings previously associated with exhibitionist dance. In acid house and connected scenes, dancing no longer solely represents the erotic display of the body. After AIDS, sexuality involves hidden dangers which leaves the body as the last refuge, but no longer safe.

All kinds of post-(acid)house predictions are inevitably being made in the wake of the fall of acid. 'New beat' from Belgium, acid jazz and deep house/garage have all been nominated as contenders. But 1989 is unlikely to see a slowing down of the accelerating speed of pop time which acid house displayed, seemingly hurtling along so quickly that it must, eventually, go backwards. 'Post' gurus like Jean Baudrillard have already told us that the 'end of the century' party is here, a decade early. Acid house shows that it is not so much a case of back to the future, as forward to the past.

13 Laager Louts and the English Disease

The summer of 1989, the last summer of the 1980s, will be memorable mainly for its pageant of late-twentieth-century racism, jingoism and nostalgia.

The recalling, and indeed obsessive celebration, of the outbreak of the anti-fascist Second World War in September 1939 throughout the mass media mingled with familiar 1970s and 1980s images of neo-Nazi English soccer hooligans stomping their way on to the continent, not to mention various cricket and rugby players trumpeting their willingness to join sports tours to the police state of South Africa. Mike Gatting, the popular tabloid cricket captain of the 'rebel' touring team, provided the sound-bites of the summer when he confessed that he did not know much about apartheid and, further, that he believed politics should be kept out of sport.

This kind of pig ignorance is a peculiarly English phenomenon. A few weeks after Gatting's homily to the press and the nation, Graham Gooch, who had led an earlier cricket tour to South Africa at the beginning of the decade and who was subsequently banned from international cricket, was appointed to captain England's own legitimate winter tour to the West Indies, uncrowned champions of the world. A previous England tour there was marked by political protest against Gooch's apartheid links. Last winter the tour to India was called off, essentially because the Essex player was the England captain.

Whether or not the 1990 Caribbean tour is similarly disrupted, it seems the height of insensitivity or stubbornness for the English cricket establishment (or, more properly, Establishment) to make such decisions. Some might think it compounded by appointing Allan Lamb, a South African qualified to play for England who regularly returns to his country of origin, as Gooch's vice-captain. Robin Smith, another South African, was probably the next name pencilled in on the team sheet by the selectors. With Zimbabwe's Graham Hick, the cricket writers' favourite son, qualifying for England in the early 1990s, what price a whole side of white South, or south, Africans representing England in the tour to Johannesburg and Cape Town (the only places in the world willing to welcome the team) in January 2000? The clutch of West Indian-born players chosen for the present England squad, including South African tour 'turncoat' Phil De Freitas, will no doubt have long been discarded by then.

What underscores the pessimism in this futuristic scenario is the lack of acute, political criticism in the English sporting media in the summer of 1989. The great West Indian cultural and political theorist, C.L.R. James, who died earlier in the year, has just had a volume of his cricket writings published by Allison and Busby. Along with *Beyond a Boundary* (James, 1996), which was written in the early 1960s in the days of West Hall, Charlie Griffith and Gary Sobers, this new collection makes clear how interlinked are writing and playing styles; and how both are part and parcel of cultural politics. By contrast, the cricket writers and broadcasters of England mirror, and ultimately sustain, the insular attitude of Gatting and Gooch.

Many of them were implicated in the behind-the-scenes disruption of England's test series against Australia by Ali Bacher and his henchmen, and have often been treated to hospitality courtesy of South African gold, both at home and abroad. During his first test match, BBC Radio 3 commentators and 'experts' openly made fun of the appearance of black Derbyshire paceman Devon Malcolm because he happens to wear glasses. The fact that the wayward Malcolm is probably the fastest bowler to play for England since Fred Trueman didn't seem to matter. What is clear is that, since the retirement of John Arlott, a noted non-Conservative, there is a paucity of critical cricket writing and broadcasting.

Football's 'boys in white' have, of course, been just as much in evidence. The most notorious incident in the summer was the hooliganism in Sweden, involving fans who travelled to watch the all-ticket World Cup qualifying match in Stockholm. Without any sense of irony, the soccer sage (and former organizer of a 'rebel' soccer tour to South Africa) Jimmy Hill dominated television studio discussion during the BBC's live coverage of the match. Full of invective for those who had taken trains and boats and planes to Scandinavia in order to display the national colours, there wasn't a single mention of the English fans' booing of every touch of the ball by John Barnes and Des Walker, England's only black players until David Rocastle came on as substitute. Match commentators similarly ignored the sickening racism of English fans. There was no analysis, either, of their *Siegheil* behaviour at the under-21 fixture between England and Sweden the night before. Past performances by England's boys on a recent trip to Iceland, or even much earlier in the decade at matches where several black players were regularly representing their country, never even figured in the television chatter.

It is hard to believe now, but the 1980s opened with confident predictions that an all-black England soccer team would be chosen before the 1990s. Dave Hill, in his book on John Barnes, *Out of his Skin* (1989), paints a horrendous picture of Merseyside racism which has prohibited black players from graduating to Anfield and Goodison from the local amateur leagues, and frequently from standing in the Kop. Everton have had only two black players in their team, and Howard Gayle, now of Blackburn Rovers, was the only other black Liverpool player before Barnes. John Barnes, though, has so far managed to negotiate successfully the racist taunts, fascists chants and thoroughly ugly gestures of Evertonians throwing bananas.

Hill could easily have gone further afield and found exactly the same levels of racism elsewhere in soccer, on and off the pitch. Old Trafford, for instance, has hardly been noted for its racial harmony, and black players – even those signed for Manchester United such as Viv Anderson – have never exactly made themselves the supporters' favourites. It remains to be seen whether new signings Danny Wallace and Paul Ince, notably fast and skilful, but also slight of build, are treated any differently once the boots go in. Whatever happens on the field, the level of police tolerance of fans' behaviour which flagrantly breaches race and public order laws at such grounds seems set to remain high well into the next decade. There is no need for new punitive soccer legislation, such as the Tory government's Football Spectators Act; a nationwide exercise of police discretion to enforce law against racism at soccer matches would be a much more effective measure.

It is to British athletics that we must look to find a more positive image of national and regional pride in English sport. Despite the blatant use by Sebastian Coe of the Barcelona World Cup and next year's Commonwealth Games to help him be selected as a prospective parliamentary candidate for the Conservative Party, athletics has become one major arena where black athletes, as well as those from the inner cities, the regions and Scotland, Northern Ireland and Wales, can hold their heads up high in front of adoring crowds and television audiences. Even Coe had to condemn 'rebel' tourists to South Africa and felt obliged to defend the way his sport celebrated values of international co-operation through sporting competition rather than the individual greed represented by apartheid and its supporters. The new breed of British athletes, Linford Christie, John Regis, Colin Jackson and Paula Dunne, shows a determination to create a different series of role models for sporting excellence while proudly pulling on their national vests, which will help to bury the memory of the Zola Budd affair (starring the *Daily Mail* and sundry other Thatcher supporters) for good.

The wartime nationalistic spirit, recalled and reworked by the media when celebrating the days of 1939, is still a crucial narrative for sport, and its presentation, today. Britain, whatever Margaret Thatcher may say, is no longer a major world power. Its Empire and Commonwealth are distant memories as far as power and control are concerned. In the savage depths of post-imperialism and deindustrialization, the first country to experience an industrial revolution and to export sports such as cricket and soccer around the world has become a talisman for racism and jingoistic fervour, especially on and around the playing field. But the media imagery surrounding sporting occasions is littered with stories of 'humiliation' at the hands of 'lesser' nations (Australia, India, Pakistan and the West Indies at cricket, for example), or else the battling spirit of the bulldog breed (cue a bloodstained Terry Butcher, or a few hundred headcases on the terraces).

In the absence of war, sport is increasingly becoming the global television event. The 1982 World Cup in Spain, following hard on the heels of the Falklands victory, married both together specularly. Watching post-Falklands national sporting teams representing England is a depressing business, made even worse by the failure of commentators to distance themselves from such a New Right version of national identity. There is no attempt on national (*sic*) television or radio to practise neutrality, or to entertain the possibility that other nations, races or people might be deserving of praise for their sporting enterprise or genius. Scottish, Irish and Welsh television viewers are simply ignored.

The 1990s are likely to see some changes, if only because the single European market of 1992, and the Channel Tunnel a year later, will bring back home a certain European identity, if not a subversion of London's sovereignty over the rest of the United Kingdom. Before then, however, we have the spectacle of the World Cup in Italy in summer 1990. Sit back for the English invasion, wallow in the nostalgia as we are forced to recall that it is twenty-four years since 'we won the cup' (under a Labour government, as Harold Wilson reminded everyone), and pray that the Mafia let Diego Maradona off the hook.

14 Moynihan Brings Out the Hooligan in Me

The much previewed Football Spectators Bill was finally unveiled by the Minister for Sport, Colin Moynihan, in January 1989. The legislation is intended, among other measures, to license a compulsory national membership card scheme for spectators at all ninety-two professional League soccer clubs in England and Wales. No one, after the spring of 1990, will be able to watch without a card, unless they fall into categories for exemption. The Thatcher government's intention to introduce such drastic measures aimed at curbing 'soccer hooliganism' has been well signalled since the aftermath of the Heysel stadium disaster in May 1985. Those of us who prophesied then that the traditional organization of professional soccer was coming to a particularly bitter end received short shrift from many of the personnel connected with the game. However, it is precisely the lack of serious preparation for the future *within* the soccer industry which has paved the way for such potentially lethal legislative intervention to be propagated. Moreover, the most traditionally conservative, aloof and autocratic bodies in the game – the Football Association and Football League – are likely to make up the bulk, if not all, of the Football Membership Authority (FMA) which will be created by the bill to administer the scheme.

Football, Law and Modernity

Much of the debate about the bill has been couched in terms of whether it will, or will not, work *technically*. Computerization and plastic ID cards are presented by the defenders of the bill as part of a long overdue process of modernization of the 'people's game' which remains (literally, in the case of many stadiums) in a 'golden age' of back-to-back terrace streets. Some of those who are opposed to the bill open themselves up to being branded as Luddites, unable to come to terms with the technological and economic changes necessary to drag this once mighty national sport and leisure business screaming into the late twentieth century. As the Thatcher government's Minister for Sport, Colin Moynihan says:

> I regret to say that there are a number of clubs who are Luddite about their approach to tackling the problems associated with the game of recent years. That isn't just the hooligan problem. It is the quality of the facilities, it's putting women's toilets into grounds, it's having a closer relationship with the local community who after all are their customers at the end of the day. It is a Luddite mentality to the development of football, lifting out of the Eighties to a national game of widespread entertainment for all groups in society, and to start picking up beyond the levels of attendance that we had five or ten years ago, let alone just getting it back up from the bottom of the U-turn, which is where we are at the present time.

Nevertheless, justifiable points have been made by critics about the dangers of trusting the new technology: for instance, that the one computerized membership card-controlled admission system already in existence has provoked the disillusionment of Plymouth Argyle, its present customer. This is dangerous ground, though, for the opponents of the bill. Teething problems with such systems may conceivably be ironed out as the remaining customers of soccer's wares become attuned to this brave new soccer world in the 1990s.

On the other hand, the exact place of this latest bill in the cluster of legal rules governing the safety and security of soccer grounds is much more telling. As Colin Moynihan argues:

> This is only part of a package of measures which have been taken over a number of years and really had behind them two very important measures. One was the Public Order Act 1986, when for the first time government concentrated on specific offences related to football hooliganism, and put measures in place to tackle them . . . And then the 1987 February agreement which was drawn up at the initiative of government, with the football authorities, to implement another package of measures ranging from local plans for the grounds and around the grounds, right the way through to closed circuit television.

These measures, together with the new bill, the minister sees as 'tiers of deterrence against hooliganism, none of which in their own right is the solution to the problem'. He perceives this problem still to be situated both inside and outside the soccer stadiums in Britain and abroad. He contends that the bill 'is one additional layer of measures which in this particular case happens to relate to the specific problem inside the grounds, and the overseas matches – because there's obviously a major problem still with the hooligan element travelling to overseas games, as we saw in West Germany last year.'

Conventional left-liberal legal criticism of the new bill has many pitfalls, despite there being numerous threatening implications for civil liberties in the proposals. Safeguards under the Data Protection Act 1984 will be available, after certain libertarian criticism was voiced to the government. Also the argument that the fan who is ejected from a ground, but not convicted of any offence, should have a right of appeal against any club ban from attending soccer, or a loss of membership, is built into the bill (a remedy not available now). In fact, the problem here is how clubs and police enforce such 'ejection' and other practices. David Phillips, assistant chief constable of Greater Manchester Police and secretary of the Association of Chief Police Officers task force on soccer hooliganism, has argued in the past that the threat of violence and vandalism disrupting local communities around soccer grounds necessitates strong police action and outweighs the concern of those same neighbourhoods with the upholding of the normal 'due process' of law. On top of this 'grey area', the new discretion to be granted to the FMA under the bill to ban from *all* grounds those who are ejected and/or banned at one club is a considerable extension of this quasi, or 'private', legal sphere.

Civil libertarian critics of this new legislation cannot afford either to ignore the frequently racist attacks on shopkeepers and householders in the vicinity of soccer grounds. Even the pilot schemes introduced by David Evans MP at his club, Luton Town, which have served as a test bed for the government's strategic thinking on soccer hooliganism, specifically addressed – at least in principle – such racist and male-dominated 'aggro' attacks on citizens. The Minister for Sport has also specifically singled out 'abhorrent racist chanting' as a major reason for needing still further legislation against soccer hooliganism.

The Rise and Fall of the 'Problem' of Football Hooliganism

If the bill is set in its proper historical and social context, it becomes easier to see it as only the most recent – if by far the most draconian – in a series of laws designed to tackle a post-1950s media-generated problem. The exact definition of the nature and scope of the problem, however, seems always tantalizingly out of reach, only referred to as something to do with the fact there is a predominantly male audience. Previous 'soccer legislation' has been notable for constructing the very problem it was said to be aimed at, and for conspicuously failing as a programme of law enforcement.

For instance, the introduction and enforcement of the Safety of Sports Grounds Act 1975, passed by a Labour government, contributed to the 'caging' in of whole sections of terrace support, and a decade-long displacement of trouble further and further away from the ground itself. Sections of the Criminal Justice (Scotland) Act 1980 have the effect not of resolving the problem of Scottish soccer violence, but of prompting new and ingenious ways of 'taking' liquor. Meanwhile, the revival of Scottish domestic soccer, and its attendance figures, in the 1980s continued as a result of other factors, both on the field and off. Further, the Sporting Events (Control of Alcohol etc.) Act 1985, passed as a panic measure after Heysel, was an equally flawed attempt to introduce south of the border the 'trial run' Scottish provisions of 1980 on banning alcohol inside, and on the way to, sports grounds. At this time, it was well recorded that the most vicious soccer gangs were those who boasted their *lack* of alcohol intake before, or around, 'big games'. The government, supported by opposition parties, persisted with the banal theory that 'drink causes soccer rowdyism', and duly implemented legislation which largely penalized the ordinary, innocent soccer fan.

This statutory legal intervention into professional soccer in particular was then stepped up a gear with the Public Order Act 1986, which, as one of its anti-hooligan measures, extended the 1985 Act to forms of transport such as transit or minibus-type vehicles. 'Football-related offences' were given a new, legal definition in the Public Order Act, and exclusion orders, in particular, were seen by the government as an effective new weapon to ban 'troublemakers'. The Fire and Safety of Places of Sport Act 1987, in addition, gave further powers to the police, such as the control over which route buses and coaches take towards and away from sports grounds.

The second part of the new bill proposes to extend the Public Order Act 1986 to those convicted of soccer-related offences by banning them from travelling overseas on days of 'designated matches'. What it cannot do is to persuade the courts to impose exclusion orders more often than they do already (only 1,089 out of 6,147 soccer-related offences resulted in orders being imposed on offenders to keep them away from soccer in the 1987–8 soccer season). Labour's Tom Pendry MP, chair of the All-Party Committee for Football, has argued that such a method of combating soccer hooliganism should be implemented effectively, and not superseded by another, potentially authoritarian statute. Pendry also points out that the 'fundamental weakness' of the new bill is that it will not change the situation where 'police rarely catch or successfully prosecute hooligans who commit acts of violence, mostly outside soccer grounds'.

It would be ironic if this much criticized bill were to provoke precisely the alliance of forces around soccer that should, in better times, have made this legislation unnecessary. The Football Supporters Association has campaigned loudly against the ID cards proposal, claiming that it is vindictive towards supporters and irrelevant to the hooligans. Two of the most astute soccer fanzine writers, Adrian Goldberg of *Off the Ball* and John Dewhirst of *City Gent*, have written critical articles in response to the minister's proposals, and soccer supporters of whatever team seem to have been uniquely united in their opposition to the bill. If the enabling bill becomes an Act and is eventually seen manifestly to fail – for instance, producing another horrific crush outside a ground such as occurred at Hillsborough in April 1989 – the new democratization movement within the game will be in a better position to push, as it does tentatively now, for supporters' representation on club boards, supporter representation on any future Football Membership Authority, and a concerted high-profile campaign to defeat racism around soccer. What is certain, though, is that this is unlikely to be the last soccer bill.

The following interview which I conducted with the Minister for Sport at the Department of the Environment on 9 January, 1989, provides a detailed justification for the bill from the point of view of the Thatcher government prior to the Hillsborough disaster. The bill was published on 17 January, 1989.

SR: Firstly, can I ask what the bill will actually be called; I've read Football Spectators, Supporters and various other things. Presumably Spectators is the accurate one, is it?

SR: Yes, it is; we can tell you that. But obviously it's not published and no details are available, but yes.

SR: And I understand it would be within the next week?

CM: Yes. It'll be – next Tuesday is the date of publication of the Bill, and literally on Tuesday we'll have the press conference in the morning, and then its introduction and then of course it'll go to the Lords.

SR: Was there any reason for it going to the Lords before the Commons?

CM: No, not really. A number of bills are introduced in the Lords. It seemed that within the organization of the parliamentary timetable it was best suited to introduction in the Lords soon after the New Year. The reason for the timing was because there was a decision made shortly before Christmas to introduce clauses to prohibit convicted hooligans from travelling abroad – that obviously needed to be worked out – by which time the parliamentary timetable in the Commons was arranged, so the best slot for it to come into parliamentary procedure was in the House of Lords. That's the reason – straightforward parliamentary organization.

SR: Presumably that will be introduced after you've met the League chairmen, which I read in the papers was also going to be next week?

CM: Yes, on that day. We felt in government that it was both right and wise to invite the League chairmen to the House of Commons in order to give them a comprehensive briefing on the provisions of the bill so that they would know first. After all, it's affecting the ninety-two League clubs. It's quite right and proper that on that day they should have a comprehensive briefing which ministers would provide.

SR: And though the League chairmen seem to have been vociferous in their opposition – if we read the newspapers correctly – what sort of things might you tell them (you say we're going to read about that next week), what sort of things might you tell them to assuage their worries, their anxieties?

CM: Well first and foremost that the scheme will be prepared by the soccer authorities and under the bill we envisage that a Football Membership Authority will be established by law. The FA and the League have jointly indicated their wish to be that FMA. If they are the FMA and they are approved by government – and we would obviously like soccer to be seen to be running its own affairs – then it would be for the FA and FL to come forward with a scheme for approval by the government. So, many of the concerns I think have been based on ignorance about how the system will work and one key point that I even found yesterday, when I was at West Ham for the game, that was misunderstood by the chairmen was it would indeed be up to soccer to come forward with the scheme.

Now, to assist them, and also to assist the press and colleagues, what I have been doing is drawing the parameters within which a scheme could operate, so when people have said to me, 'Well, what is the sort of technology that can be used?', then I would say, 'This is the type of technology that is available.' But of course it will be up to soccer to look at what it sees as being the best technology to deliver a scheme within the parameters outlined in the bill. And that's effectively what the bill will be – an enabling measure; approximately 50 per cent of the bill will be licensing arrangements for grounds where designated matches will be played, coupled with the establishment of the FMA, what we see as the conditions required to run a national membership scheme, like proper access to the ground, the proper control and monitoring of membership cards, and that will formulate 50 per cent and the new criminal offences associated with those controls. The other 50 per cent of the bill will concentrate on measures to be taken to prohibit those convicted of soccer-related offences under the 1986 Public Order Act from travelling overseas on days of designated matches, and that is a substantial proportion of the bill, so I'm pre-empting a little bit since I haven't actually briefed any other colleagues on it yet in the press world. Effectively the bill is divided into those two important parts, part A and part B, and I see both as very important indeed.

The other point that I have made to them to assuage their concerns, and I think that the first point that I made is extremely important – if soccer is actually sitting down and proposing a scheme within remit of the law, then obviously they have the opportunity to assuage their own concerns when they're drawing up details of the proposed scheme.

The other point I'd make, which I think is a very important one, this is only part of a package of measures that have been taken over a number of years and really had behind them two very important measures. One was the Public Order Act 1986, when for the first time government concentrated on specific offences related to soccer hooliganism, and put measures in place to tackle them – a whole range of measures (not just the attendance orders, detention orders – exclusion orders particularly with regard to soccer – but the other two had a bearing on soccer) – and defined what a soccer-related offence was. And then the 1987 February agreement which was drawn up at the initiative of government, with the soccer authorities, to implement another package of measures ranging from local plans for the grounds and around the grounds, right the way through to closed-circuit television – and the importance is that clearly as an important deterrent, closed-circuit television is critical – and outside the grounds. With this package of measures related to the 1986 Public Order Act you have, as it were, tiers of deterrence against hooliganism, none of which in their own right is the solution to the problem, but all of which add up to a package of deterrence, a package of measures to deter the hooligan element.

And so I firmly believe that the problem should be addressed both inside and outside the grounds and indeed overseas, which is why this specific bill that we are now talking about is one additional layer of measures which in this particular case happens to relate to the specific problem inside the grounds, and the overseas matches – because there's obviously a major problem still with the hooligan element travelling to overseas games, as we saw in West Germany last year.

So there was an inevitable press concentration on the national membership scheme, but the wise observer of the problem of soccer hooliganism will realize that in fact the way government and soccer jointly are tackling the problem, is a series of measures to tackle the problem wherever it exists, ranging from increased power to the British Transport Police through to exclusion orders through to the Home Secretary writing to magistrates about tougher sentencing, from cases of hooliganism outside the grounds, which he did earlier this year, to closed-circuit television, national membership schemes, effective segregation, better policing outside the grounds, better policing inside the grounds, greater intelligence between international forces, greater intelligence between police forces inside this country. And there has been far more monitoring in the last twelve months with police forces actually sending 'spotters' to away games, which again we didn't have three or four years ago. So it is that package of measures that I think is important and it is a point that I certainly will be emphasizing when I meet the soccer authorities.

SR: Presumably we would expect them, understanding those things, to be in support of such measures. Certainly, publicly, they've gone on record in the past supporting anti-soccer hooligan measures. Presumably their worries may be technological, it may be the technical aspects. What would you say to them about the technology which they've started to worry about?

CM: It was interesting because again going round to the matches (take yesterday at West Ham) the main concerns were specific technical concerns. In fact to the exclusion of all other concerns, yesterday, interestingly enough, and when I spoke to the police at all levels the police concerns were – the only question I had (otherwise they were in favour of the national membership scheme) the only question I had was a technical question, from the police as well, not just the soccer authorities, questions about what happens if there is computer downtime during the last ten minutes before the match starts? What happens if there are large crowds coming to a turnstile just before a game starts, is it going to slow down entry? How is stewarding going to be affected or altered? Some questions are even: do we have to have complete new turnstiles?

But to answer those questions: throughout this debate so far there are very clear, comprehensive answers to all of those, which the moment one expresses them and puts them to the critics allay their concerns. For example: because of the licensing system, whereby all grounds for designated matches will be licensed, if the computer breaks down, which we don't anticipate it will but we've got to look at that possibility, then everybody is let in just as they are now. If, however, you are involved in a fight inside the ground then because that ground is licensed under the national membership scheme all the sanctions of the national membership scheme apply. So somebody who is arrested, found guilty by the courts and sentenced for five years, then the five-year ban will continue to apply despite the fact that his card didn't actually need to light up a particular machine because of computer downtime just before the game started. Equally the technology is clearly available now for just as swift an entry into the grounds as currently exists. Indeed, the only thing that slows down entering the grounds is paying cash, or making sure that you hand something over to the turnstile operator who then has to look at it and hand it back to you, be it a ticket or even a season ticket. The technology is available for you to actually touch a small pad on the outside of the grille so you don't actually have to hand anything over at all, you can continue to walk through, touch this pad and no time is lost whatsoever, and indeed potentially that could be used as a direct debit facility, so you wouldn't even need to hand out cash whereas you had previously done so. David Miller did a piece on that in *The Times* last week which is worth looking at.

SR: I was interested in that because he is the only person I know of who mentioned the direct debit issue and nobody else has raised it. I understand what you're saying, but what if, say, Plymouth Argyle's chairman says to you 'Our system put in by Aquix Ltd has not been satisfactory.' What is the answer to that?

CM: Well, the answer to that is that the right technology for the scheme is to be chosen by the Football Membership Authority. There is certainly no intention of the government to appoint a specific company, and quite rightly there are ninety-one out of ninety-two schemes already in operation, partial membership schemes. It must be right that that pool of information and expertise, the League clubs, get together and say to the FA and the League who are forming the company – this is what they're talking about – whether or not is up to them. Their intention is at the moment to form a company to form the FMA, to say to the FMA 'The technology for this is the most appropriate technology, is Technology X or Technology Y'. There is a whole range. We've had over a hundred different companies, and it's not been my intention to say one particular technology is better than another, simply that the more advanced the technology – if you look at the GEC technology, for example, there is technology available that will lead to no delays at the turnstiles. It is up to the FMA to decide whether they choose that technology for recommendation to the government.

SR: And there are other European countries (Spain for example) who have tried that and seem to claim that the technology is there. It seems to be 'Luddism', doesn't it?

CM: I think in this day and age there is no doubt whatsoever that the technology is available for a swift, effective, technically competent system of checking a card, especially since you're not checking against a file of everybody going into every ground; you're only checking it against a referral file of those banned. Therefore, if you have a new card say every three years, we don't anticipate that we're going to have tens of thousands of people banned. The referral file will be pretty small, that will be an instant pick-up. If you were checking against all members to make sure your card was one of a valid sector of everybody else in soccer, of course it's going to take time for the computer to work that one out, but if you're just talking about those who are banned on your referral file, which all companies we've spoken to have stated, then it is quite clear that can then be an extremely swift and efficient procedure; and it isn't just the Spanish. Interestingly enough, the Dutch also are currently looking at a similar system, so the technology is there. What is important is for soccer to look at the most appropriate technology for the requirements of the scheme.

SR: And it is something that professional soccer in this country seems to have been slow in modernizing its own house for many years on all sorts of issues – safety, security and so on – and this is another one, isn't it?

CM: Well, there are still clubs that haven't got closed-circuit television in, despite the fact they don't have to pay for it, as the soccer trust are paying for the closed-circuit television installation in the grounds, so there's no cost incurred whatsoever, and despite the fact that it is universally agreed that a closed-circuit television camera moving above the heads of a section of the crowd is a deterrent to people getting involved in a scrap. Even if there's no film in it, the very presence of that camera is a deterrent.

Fortunately there *are* films in them all and they are developing now from black and white to colour, which is also a great help to the police. But there are still clubs in the League that do not have closed-circuit television in. There are still clubs that I've written to time and again that still haven't put it in. You use the word 'Luddite'. I regret to say that there are a number of clubs who are Luddite about their approach to tackling the problems associated with the game over the recent years. That isn't just the hooligan problem. It is the quality of the facilities, it's putting women's toilets into the grounds, it's having a close relationship with the local community who after all are their customers at the end of the day. It is a Luddite mentality to the development of soccer, lifting it out of the Eighties to a national game of widespread entertainment for all groups in society, and to start picking up beyond the levels of attendance that we had five or ten years ago, let alone just getting it back up from the bottom of the U-turn, which is where we are at the present time.

So I really do think that it is to a great extent an attitude of mind of soccer to modernize itself and ask itself where it wants to be in ten years. If it takes no action against the hooligan element then there can be no guarantee that the problems we saw at the Chelsea match at the end of the last season, the Scarborough match at the beginning, the problems in Europe and the Heysel problems will not occur again. Until we find an effective way to separate the hooligan from the true soccer supporter not only will we have a continuation of the problems both inside and outside the grounds, we won't get families coming back and people coming back who currently are just too frightened to go to soccer. Time and time again we come across 'Well, I'm not going to take my grandson to soccer' and that's tragic for the game, let alone for 'law and order', and this can be a mechanism whereby the future of the game is secured.

SR: How would you characterize that hooligan problem, because in fifteen years it's been there hasn't it, and we might say that it's been there for a hundred years, but the modern problem, the modern soccer hooligan, has been there for twenty-five years. How would you characterize it now?

What is it that is the problem for the father who won't take his son, the grandfather who won't take his grandson, and so on?

CM: It can be categorized in a number of ways. Undoubtedly there is a general climate of aggression which is a major factor in putting off a lot of people from going to soccer. It is a climate of aggression for people even going about their normal Saturday afternoon shopping in the vicinity of soccer grounds, and it is one that is associated with almost a euphoric, tribal reaction that has been certainly affected by drink, alcohol, which seems in many cases almost to numb normal behaviour – people get involved in a crowd, they get carried away with euphoria, there's the chanting that goes with that, much of it abhorrent racist chanting, and in that crowd they lose the sense of responsibility and a very strong aggressive instinct is fuelled by alcohol frequently, and that in turn literally worries very large numbers of people from going anywhere near a soccer match. Now, that only relates to a very small proportion of people who go along to soccer, but it inevitably means that the majority of the rest of those of us who love soccer and go along are men, though not the families – the families' enclosures are still a very small proportion of grounds round the country, they're actually identified as one small enclosure in most grounds. The number of women who go to soccer is disproportionately small compared to other sports, and indeed to other countries. And that is one group.

Now there is undoubtedly also the hardcore criminal element and I think this is the area that, certainly in terms of policing of soccer, has been recognized more clearly than it was ten, fifteen and twenty years ago when we had the beginning of these problems. The 'firms' are often managed by families. The running of them is in a very highly sophisticated, hierarchical structure. Often the people who have started a lot of the problems have been sitting in the comfortable seats indicating to others to start a movement down the terraces, and there are people who in no way go to soccer to become involved in a punch-up or whatever who are aggravated and become involved in fighting. In other words, it is a highly developed criminal element and the police have learned a great deal about that element over the last literally three or four years, no more than that. It is an international network for this element. The meetings between rival groups of people who are in the criminal world of soccer hooliganism, respected by each other, are known to take place and are commonplace at overseas matches, and I think that we should therefore recognize that there are the two very distinct groups. And I've read endless sociological papers by people who are far more expert than we are in government of assessing this, who very clearly identify a hardcore criminal group.

SR: But you could say those people were also there – you're implying those people were also there – over the last twenty years, in a sense . . .

CM: I think it's become a more sophisticated criminal group.

SR: Yes, I was going to ask you whether you think it's actually worse now than say in the early 1980s or even in the 1970s, when these people were . . .

CM: Yes, I do. I think it's different, and I think it's been shown to be different particularly with regard to the overseas travelling. I mean that's where it really comes to the fore, and that is where the – it was there before then, never there to the developed, criminal extent which the police have clearly identified exists today, and that in turn has led to the 'spotters' moving around from club to club, and that in turn has led to far greater police intelligence, and that in turn has concentrated the minds of ministers at the European Council of Ministers for Sport, and this specific issue was raised for the first time only last year.

SR: In a sense some of your critics really, given what they see as problems with the bill, are hoist on their own petard, because in the past they haven't done anything, government hasn't done, in the 1970s and perhaps up to the mid-1980s, we haven't done anything about precisely that problem, and perhaps it's inaction which has led to things being 'worse'.

CM: Yes, I think that for twenty-five years there has been inadequate realization of just how severe this problem is, not in Britain, this problem had become international, and quite rightly governments of all political complexions have always preferred the governing bodies of sport to put their own house in order. Too frequently the soccer authorities have been perceived to take no or ineffective action, where Oxley of the Rugby League takes determined and immediate action, where Hopkin of the British Boxing Board of Control immediately intervenes, when there's a problem – like Sibson's fight which I was at last year – and immediately implements new measures. And with reports on major incidents in the domestic game inside the grounds such as the Chelsea pitch invasion last year, no report was received by this office until into the next session; not a matter of a few days, it was a matter of months before a report was received. Equally indiscipline on the pitch in other sports: an exceptionally tough line is taken because they recognize that in a high-media-profile world a lot of the youngsters look up to the top sportsmen as people who are their heroes and heroines, and if rackets are thrown at Wimbledon there are kids who will imitate by example; and against the cynical foul, the 'professional foul', punch-ups on the pitch – there was another one yesterday – a punch-up on the pitch. There has needed to be over this twenty-five years very tough and determined action taken by the FA and the League, as there has been by other governing bodies. But there hasn't been.

SR: Why soccer rather than these other sports? Is it back to them not wanting to be bothered?

CM: I think you're tracing a line, a legacy of soccer, which is almost unique to soccer. And that is the tradition of highly successful, local, influential people going on to the boards of their local soccer clubs; a deeply parochial attitude within each club that has rejected the direct control of even its own governing body, the League. It has rejected direct intervention by the League or the FA to the point when the League – and we've seen this in the last six months, it's a very interesting reflection of it – the League by comparison to governing bodies in other sports is remarkably weak, retains minimal power over the clubs, indeed the FA handle most of the powers that can be exercised as you know over soccer, and the net result of that is nothing more than a reflection of evolution in the soccer game which has centred very much on the individual club being almost a 'laager' of its own, and often within very strong family ties, but very parochial in outlook, and not wishing anybody – be it the FA, the League or the government or any outside agent – to what it perceives to be interference with the running of their club. Now that doesn't apply in any other sport, right across the board of the 200-plus sports in this country, governing bodies that I know. It doesn't apply in any other sport, and I think that that is a real difficulty for those who are enlightened in soccer administration and who are in the League and do want to see change.

SR: Is that why you feel that it is necessary to make it a Football Bill and not a Sports Bill, or is it that you see soccer as the problem, because there are more soccer hooligans than there are, say, cricket hooligans?

CM: Yes. Effectively the problem that exists within soccer – and again this isn't domestic, it's international – the problem that exists in soccer with their hooligan element is totally out of proportion to any other sport. If there was a similar level, if we had 6,000 arrests in rugby league or boxing or angling or women's hockey or racing and the incidents of violence which have been particularly visible on the television screens, regrettably week after week, both nationally and internationally, then it would be the duty of the government to take action for that sport.

SR: Could you not say that, say, in rugby league? I talk to the north-west police who say that increasingly over the last few years there have been more problems within rugby league than there were a decade ago. With something like, not so much test match cricket but in one-day cricket, like the one in Birmingham where in fact soccer fans *were* involved, is the danger not that, if you succeed in having a law which is efficient and enforced well, you displace the problem to places like cricket matches which at the moment are underpoliced? I mean I've been to Old Trafford, for example, where the cricket authorities have been very wary about that problem. They haven't had to deal with it because it hasn't really come on to them yet. Is it not possible that it may do as a result of a more effective bill now?

CM: I can only answer the way I envisage it will happen, and my answer to you is that the only indication is that if you don't have all the criteria that go towards a group of soccer hooligans rioting or being involved in a fight, and I mentioned many of them earlier, if you don't have all those then you don't have the violence. Now, there will inevitably be a very small hardcore criminal element that currently focuses its attention on soccer and may start focusing its attention on smashing shop windows in a high street. If there is that small element – and I hope there isn't, but if it is inevitable that there is that very small percentage – then the law must tackle that problem wherever it exists. What I do not believe is that that group will displace itself and go to another sport. It doesn't in the off season of soccer. If it did then I'd be more concerned about the possibility of that.

It just doesn't. The incidents that have actually occurred in other sports take place during the soccer season – admittedly that early cricket match, the Birmingham one, was an example in point – but it just doesn't displace itself so that the incidence of violence increases proportionately at other sporting events. But I'm absolutely convinced of the argument that if there was ever the scale, and I do not believe it will happen, that if there was the scale of hooliganism associated with another sport in the country, it would be the duty of government to come to Parliament and bring forward the appropriate measures.

SR: You did choose, as I understand it, to leave aside those other sports?

CM: I did, but it is more than that reason. I'm a firm believer in the prerogative of Parliament to assess measures for specific conditions for specific instances. I do not believe that it makes good legislation to grant wide powers to a Secretary of State without recourse to Parliament. Therefore, if Parliament decides that tough action of this form needs to be taken on soccer, I do not believe it right to ask Parliament at the same time to give the Secretary of State powers to cover any other sport at any other time in the future. If there is a problem that merits parliamentary consideration for further law, then ministers have a duty to go to Parliament. So it's actually quite a strong political principle at stake there.

There is a second point, but this is less important, and that is that what is right for one sport is not necessarily right for another. A national membership scheme in a clearly defined area with specific access can be very effective in separating the soccer hooligan from the true supporter. A national membership scheme on Epsom Downs for Derby Day would be completely irrelevant because you can just walk on to Epsom Downs from whichever side you like. So one would require appropriate measures if there was ever, and I just don't believe there will be – there's no international indication, there's no historical indication – that there would ever be the scale of problems associated with hooliganism at any other sport.

SR: One thing that, if you like, the ordinary, 'innocent', non-hooligan fan puts to you through an organization like the Football Supporters' Association, but also through people who've never been involved in trouble who have spoken out, is why should soccer be picked out on the basis of, say, 6,000 arrests during the 1987–8 season when there is a much more general problem of crime in the country? Can I ask you about the 6,000 for a minute, the 6,147 or whatever there was in 1987–8, that were soccer-related offences? One of those ordinary soccer fans' arguments is that pick-pocketing, ticket-touting, that sort of offence, would also come within soccer-related offences in those figures. How would the bill – they can see how the bill might stop soccer-related offences within the ground, but they can't see how those other soccer-related offences within the 6,000 would be stopped.

CM: Well, because anybody under the 1986 Public Order Act who is found guilty by the courts of any offence within the Public Order Act which is defined in law as soccer-related would be liable to loss of membership either of two or five years, depending on the severity of the offence. Effectively, the bill will suggest that somebody who goes into prison will be banned for five years. So certainly I want to stop people thieving at soccer matches just as I want to stop people hitting each other, or any of the crimes that lead the police to take action, and we don't want those people in soccer matches.

SR: But could that not already be done? You mentioned in the Public Order Act 1986. Could that not already be under Part 4 and the exclusion order? I mean, I read – again I'm not sure that the statistics are right – but out of that 6,000 about 1,000, slightly more than 1,000, exclusion orders were issued by the courts. Is there not a problem of the courts' discretion, not enforcing it, as perhaps ministers would have liked?

CM: It is an extension of that, the exclusion orders, and undoubtedly I would like to see and government would like to see at the moment the exclusion orders extended, and this is a method of so doing. There's a far more important point about the Football Membership Authority, and that is currently there are thousands of people who do not come before the courts, but who are ejected from grounds and who are banned from individual grounds, who find themselves able to do two things, to have two choices. One thing is as far as ejections are concerned, and if you talk about the distinction between arrest and ejections, yesterday was, I shall give you precise figures, but yesterday was of the order of 5 arrests and 81 ejections, so you've got 5 arrests and 81 ejections – those ejections don't come before the courts. Those people who have been ejected from the ground and taken police time and trouble to be ejected, and caused an affray sufficient to be ejected, will now be able to be banned from going to any one of the ninety-two grounds, without conviction, and this is because we're giving discretionary powers to the Football Membership Authority, which will be the soccer clubs, the people who are banning them at the moment. At the moment all that happens is that they walk around the side and they come back in again, and some of them will pay £24 – they'll go four times round and pay £6 and come back again – and the police know it happens. They've ejected them and they go straight the way round, and if they didn't go round to see their own team play, they can go to another club. Technically it is possible for West Ham to phone up all the other ninety-one clubs and say, 'These are the hundreds of people who we happen to have decided to ban from our club. Can you ban them as well?' And after all, there's no good reason why any soccer fan who's a sufficient trouble maker to be banned from one club can't be banned from going to any other, so the FMA will have discretionary powers, outside the courts, discretionary powers to ban people for the same period of time as the courts will have.

SR: But there would be, and presumably their membership cards would be confiscated?

CM: Well, they don't really need to do that, as long as they've got the name. I don't know if you've seen what happens. I've just seen it yesterday. There are people brought in, they take their shoes off, they get their names and addresses, photograph of them, and they'll eject them. It's not an arrest, the people are ejected. So out of the ground they've gone and they've got the name, you don't actually need to take their card from them, you simply programme into the computer, the local computer just as you can now, the name and number if you've had a look at the card but not otherwise, of the guy concerned and he's banned from every ground. If he tries to come in with his card, he's banned from every ground. You are, therefore, not just tackling those who are covered by the orders, you are actually tackling all the people that the soccer clubs have decided that they don't want inside their own grounds, and it will be the Football League and the FA who decide on those that they don't want coming into their grounds, just as they can now. It's an extension of what they can do now, but it's far more effective – comprehensive extension of banning all those that they regard as troublemakers inside the grounds now – and obviously there must be an appeal mechanism.

SR: I am going to say, presumably some aspect of natural justice would have to come in, wouldn't it?

CM: After all, you might be mistaken. It might be a case of mistaken identity.

SR: And they haven't been convicted. Surely that's one of the problems?

CM: Well no, because what happens now. There's a lot of people who haven't been convicted who are banned by a club.

SR: But is that not one of the reasons why perhaps there is a disquiet about the civil liberties issue? Although the soccer chairmen are mainly worrying about technology, even they might worry a bit about people who have been ejected but not convicted. There is a kind of stigma which is only on the say-so of a policeman throwing you out, and one of the things that is obvious in research into policing is that a lot of police forces – certainly in the north-west – would say ejection figures are actually more important than arrest figures. We can say that the real trouble-makers, the real 'bad games' for us, are ones where ejection figures are high rather than arrest figures, and it's a difficult legal issue, isn't it, that people who've been ejected, ordinary citizens, will say 'Why aren't they then convicted?'

CM: Well, as a politician who is a strong libertarian, I have a considerable degree of sympathy with that. For that reason we are building – we're pre-empting the bill here – my colleagues around here aren't too worried about that, so I will brief you fully. But that is why it struck me that whilst these discretionary powers are very important for the FMA to have them, it would be difficult to sustain an argument which allowed the FMA – even if it was soccer – to ban people for ten or twenty years, whereas somebody who'd been put inside was only going to be banned for five. I want to err even more cautiously on the ejections and those who were banned, by saying to the FMA that there should be a maximum two-year ban and if somebody who's not gone before the courts but is a known troublemaker, has persistently caused trouble, then that club would have to apply to the FMA every two years for that to be renewed. Now that's one point, but second, and very important, is there must be an appropriate appeal mechanism against that and that is built into the bill. So those are two areas that are built in to protect the civil liberties of individuals against the FMA exercising discretionary powers which they could actually do now. So it is a greater safeguard and in fact . . .

SR: Because there isn't one now?

CM: No, because you can be banned for twenty years now.

SR: So would it be a (I'm asking about the bill) but would it be a sub-committee of the FMA, would it be for them to decide?

CM: I'm going to have to wait for that, it will not be them to decide. In the first instance, they will have to review any appeal that comes to them, but then we'll have an additional appeal mechanism. It is terribly important that there is an appeal mechanism which is separate from those who are deciding on the punishment. There is one other very important thing that hasn't come through and that is the Data Protection Act. A number of people have been concerned about the potential for mass direct mailing immediately they've become a member of the scheme. Whilst it is obvi-ously the case that the only mail you'll receive are from sponsors of your club, if you have a club allegiance or from the national membership scheme if you have no club allegiance – and the vast majority of people do have club allegiance – and whilst the fact is that you may only have three or four sponsors of the scheme, whoever's got their logo on your card who happens to be attached to Reading because they've got British Rail sponsoring, so you are therefore unlikely to get a large amount of post.

Whilst that is factually the case, I still think the individual should have an additional right not to receive direct mail if that individual doesn't wish it to be used in that commercial fashion. For that reason we will be taking the option – and it isn't one that we have to take – of being fully party to the Data Protection Act, and that means that at the request of the Registrar on the form will be a cross or box for you as a potential member of the national membership scheme to indicate you do not wish to receive mail shots from the club which you have joined, or if you haven't joined a club through the national membership scheme. Clearly that is to the economic disadvantage, the commercial disadvantage of your club, and I think the vast majority of people would be told by their clubs well in advance that we're only having one sponsor and we would like you to receive direct mail from that sponsor, but I still think even then that it must be right to allow the individual member to decide whether or not he wishes to receive that.

SR: Just lastly on that, this is still presumably outside the Data Protection Act? The information about the member would still not be able to be looked at, would it?

CM: Yes it would, by the member, not by anybody else. All the principles of the Data Protection Act are going to apply because we – not because they have to – simply because the government has decided that that should be a condition of the national membership scheme to protect individual liberty. The interesting point about the bill – I mean you'll be able to examine this in detail next week – the interesting point about the bill is it actually protects individual liberties more than currently exists for the soccer supporter, who can be thrown out of the ground and kept out of the ground, and that to me is very important especially where we are asking everybody to carry a national membership card in order to divide the hooligan from the soccer supporter, and I think that once this is actually implemented there will be a substantial increase over the years of people coming back to soccer.

To begin with there will be a small proportion who will not get their cards even though they've got twelve months to get it and who may suddenly think 'I might go to soccer', realize they haven't got a national membership card, not want to go down an hour early – it's only a very small number of people – or on the morning of the game, and get a card. For each one of those, the millions who used to go to soccer, who currently don't realize now they can go in safety and if all the other points I made earlier about a different approach by the clubs, recognizing all the various challenges that exist with regard to a close relationship with their customers rather than regard them as turnstile fodder, having curtain-raisers, having the kids playing in divisions earlier in the day so the parents are much more involved, because the schools are much more involved with the clubs. If all these initiatives get off the ground and they are imaginative in looking forward then you'll get many more people coming back to soccer in ten years' time than there are now.

Photographs by **Patrick Henry**

Index

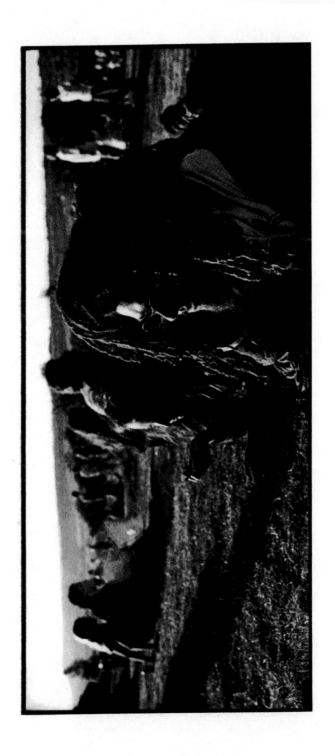

15 Supertifo

By the end of the 1990 matches, the last four World Cup Finals will all have been staged in Latin countries: Argentina in 1978 where the host country won, Spain in 1982 where Italy won, and Mexico in 1986 where the 'Hand of God' helped Argentina on their way to victory. The forthcoming spectacle in Italy this summer has already received considerable media hype, but whether or not Italy go on to win the coveted trophy for a record fourth time, the triumph of Italian style and fashion is already assured.

In Britain, the media's version of the story of the World Cup tradition-ally stages the Finals through a grand dualism, broadly organizing the major footballing powers into two camps – the Latins and the Europeans. This classic opposition provides a popular mythology, drawing on cultural stereotypes and tactical approaches, which informs press and television coverage, constructing an entertaining pantomime where instinct meets discipline, consistency opposes temperament and teamwork encounters showmanship. While in the political arena, notions of 'Latin-ness' are commonly denigrated, in a sporting context these characteristics are frequently celebrated.

The position that Italy occupies within the distinction between Latins and Europeans is somewhat contradictory. Italy is perceived as culturally the natural ally of Brazil, Argentina and Spain, yet it is tactically more defen-sively minded on the soccer field than its Latin counterparts (despite Brazil's recent conversion to the *libero*, or sweeper), and typically operates a *catenaccio* system of man-to-man marking, more in line with European soccer style. England, on the contrary, persistently refuses to adopt a sweeper system at national level, despite some British clubs' experiments, and maintains a perverse notion of wingers as the route to soccer style and flair at the very time all other national teams are seemingly abandoning them. England's insistence on this specific soccer style has compounded its position on the margins of Europe, a kind of self-emposed exile, spurred on by the UEFA ban since Heysel. Curiously, it was England's successful 1966 World Cup win at Wembley that marked the demise of wing play in the international game.

This contradiction of 'Italian-ness' is evident in the extensive build-up to the *Mondiali*, which turns to the extravagant aspects of a Latin nation that values and exults cultural institutions like soccer and opera, without the high culture/low culture division employed in Britain. The privileged position which soccer enjoys in Italian society has provided considerable emphasis for the dramatic aspects of the 'Italia 90' sales pitch, with short promo films on each of the twelve cities staging the matches directed by top-name film-makers such as Fellini, Rosi and Bertolucci, poster design by Italy's most acclaimed living artist, Burri, and theme music from Giorgio Moroder – in sharp contrast to England's signature tune, 'World in motion' penned and performed by New Order. Moreover, the crescendo to the greatest event on earth will be provided by a televised open-air concert which will bring together the world's most renowned tenors, Pavarotti, Domingo and Carreras. Who knows, they may even offer us a rendition of the winning Italian entry for the Eurovision Song Contest *Insieme*!

The elevated status of soccer in Italy is also reflected in the fan culture surrounding the game. Soccer in Italy constantly pervades the airwaves, with back-to-back live televised games from different countries a commonplace occurrence. A much wider cross-section of the population avidly follows soccer in Italy than in Britain: for instance, many more women spectators attend games and there are also women's professional soccer teams. Moreover, the consumption of the event is often spectacular. *Supertifo* (Superfan), an Italian monthly soccer magazine which started in 1985 – the year of the Heysel disaster where thirty-nine spectators, mainly Juventus fans, were crushed to death – offers a vivid account of the young soccer scene in Italy. By means of words and lavish colour photography it focuses on the traditionally (in Britain) 'invisible' space of soccer watching – on the way to the game, organizing the *curva* (terraces) before the game, the spectacle during the game (the 'match within a match' between rival *tifosi*). A panoply of smoke bombs, banners, huge flags, horns and scarves accompanies the sensational event that is Italian soccer watching.

Since the 1960s in England, such space has been subject to much more stringent surveillance from the soccer authorities, law and the police than in continental western Europe, notwithstanding various inflatable and dressing-up crazes among English fans in the last few seasons. Clubs like the Hacienda in Manchester now transport themselves, and their soccer and music clientele, on monthly jaunts to Europe in a desperate search for space and spectacle which is increasingly being denied them in the United Kingdom. For instance, the Entertainments (Increased Penalties) Bill – dubbed the 'Acid House Bill' in the popular press – threatens to criminalize the 'right to party', and compounds the recent changes in the licensing laws which makes it easier for the police to object to legal clubs being granted licences. All of this has spawned an unexpected exodus of new, young diplomats, prospecting for a stylish Euro-citizenship in marked preference to what is on offer in poll tax-ridden, post-imperial Britain. Moreover, since 1985 the Thatcher government has unleashed a ferocious onslaught on soccer in England. But the 'English disease' which allegedly plagues the soccer industry has comprised styles of chanting, singing and fighting which now reverberate around other European countries such as Holland and West Germany. Styles of dress and haircuts on the continent regularly feature throwbacks to the English hooligan styles of the late 1960s and early 1970s, such as skinhead subcultural fashions, Union Jack flags and t-shirts, and the wearing of knotted soccer scarves around the neck or wrist.

While the British media's account of World Cup preparations in Italy has been dominated by the prospect of violence, anticipated in the much-heralded media story of the meeting between Dutch and English fans in Sardinia, British domestic youth culture has primed itself for other possibilities for the Finals, with magazines such as *The Face*, *i-D*, *Blitz* and *Arena* succumbing to the Latin promise of theatre, spectacle and carnival. Soccer trade magazines in Britain (*Shoot*, *Match*, *Football Monthly*, *World Soccer* and newcomers like *Inside Football*) have never been the epitome of style, just as footballers' haircuts have always been widely ridiculed in soccer fanzine culture. The seductive influence which Italian-style fashion holds is made manifest as *The Face* has us 'knitting up for the World Cup' with revamped Buffalo Boy Barry Kamen as Italian soccer casual. Its male audience offshoot *Arena* asks 'why the Italians have the best soccer shirts' despite the zany array of British club away kits. The influence which Italian designer fashion has wielded since the late 1970s remains and now feeds into the larger phenomenon of *sport couture* alongside black American street styles. From the birth of the casual in the 1978–9 soccer season, following a series of sorties into Europe to follow their teams by soccer fans in Merseyside, Manchester, London and Scotland, where Italian and other styles were (literally and metaphorically) ripped out of their European context, there has been a national style revolution. During the 1980s it became permissible for 'youth' (young and old, female *and* male) to be interested in fashion on a scale undreamt of in the 1960s and 1970s. It is worth remembering that the present over-hyped media focus on 'scally' culture – flared jeans, The Farm, Happy Mondays, Stone Roses – began over a decade ago when *The Face* was still selling us all club culture via Culture Club and Boy George.

In the 1990s, much British youth culture increasingly looks to a European milieu rather than North America. The emergence of a Euro-clubbing scene over the last few years is strong evidence of this trend. It was prematurely signalled by the Pet Shop Boys, in the mid-1980s, celebrating the *paninaro* look which mixed Italian casual wear and 1950s American retro, and gained fuller recognition with the success of Italian Euro-disco and house, and the more general context of *casa Latina*. 'Latin-ness'[1], and in particular 'Italian-ness', now has an established place in British pop culture as never before. It is this which marks out the 1990 World Cup in Italy in June and July as a major global event underscored by style and fashion. Enjoy it while you can. The next World Cup is held in 1994 in the United States of America: this could be the *last* World Cup before the tournament turns into a game of four halves and a gladiatorial battle conducted for prime-time television.

PART III

CLUBCULTURES

16 Oh Madchester, So Much to Answer For

Manchester in the summer of 1992 began what looks like a whole decade of celebrating the culturally regenerated, new European, post-industrial, postmodern cityscape. Ever since 'Madchester' hit the cover of *Newsweek* in the summer of 1990, the mass media spindoctors have had a field day. Olympic Bid 2000, Year of Drams 1994, In the City music seminar, Metrolink, Boddington's Manchester Festival of TV and the Arts, yuppie flats and gentrification: you name it. Hyperreal Manchester! What we must not forget among all the selling of the 'image' of this overgrown urban jungle is that, at a national and international level these days, there is precious little left to sell in the world but our 'heritage': the past, rather than manufactured goods, is what makes our deindustrializing economic world go round. We even have a new government ministry dedicated to it.

One significant result of John Major's Conservative Party victory at the polls on 9 April 1992 was the creation of a new Department of National Heritage – labelled already as the 'Ministry of Fun' – under the tutelage of the MP for Putney, David Mellor, eventually forced to resign by a media onslaught over the summer months about various aspects of his private life. An influential sidekick of John Major since the anti-Thatcher coup in November 1990, not to mention – now infamously as the subject of the Chelsea fans' chant 'There's only one David Mellor' – a fellow soccer supporter, the new Secretary of State proclaimed on his appointment that alongside the serious enterprise of wealth creation in the new Conservative age there should be room for some measure of pleasure and culture – in short, 'fun'. Life, *contra* Margaret Thatcher, in the 1990s United Kingdom was not entirely to be about making money. The new, lightly staffed, *sans* Mellor department encompasses apparently disparate, but collectively important, areas of national cultural life, such as parks, heritage, tourism, 'arts', film, sport and, of course, broadcasting. Some of these cultural fields have lacked any previous cabinet representation, and their elevation into sharper political focus is to be welcomed. The much-touted national lottery also comes under the brief of the Heritage ministry.

All three major parties had similar kinds of proposals in their manifesto packages, but the Conservatives, arguably, had the most developed and comprehensive structural programme, reminiscent, however slightly and unintentionally, of the French Ministry for Culture and Communication under Jack Lang, which is distinguished by its commitment to public spending on the arts and culture. Defeat at the general election meant that the British Labour Party will not yet have the chance to emulate and develop the seeds of the Big (French) Idea contained in its own manifesto commitment to a Ministry for Culture. The Tory approach, though, seems destined to continue the New Right free-market policies of the 1980s which have created so many long-term difficulties for the business of cultural production and consumption, without recognizing the widespread acceptance of a rather different, self-regulating but to some extent mutually co-operative, business and enterprise culture in the cultural industries such as popular music, video and fan magazine publishing, which already flourishes.

The creation of a new government department responsible for 'leisure' and 'culture' raises two major questions. One is the new concentration of statutory and other powers for regulation of the diverse aspects of what Frankfurt School theorist Theodor Adorno once called The Culture Industry. The other is the specific nature of the pleasure and leisure business in Conservative Britain in the 1990s. For instance, legislation on the mass media is inevitable before the 1997 general election, as the BBC's charter falls due for renewal in 1995 – prompting an alternative Tory title for the Heritage Department as the 'Ministry of Free Kicks'; which the party knows Mellor's successor Peter Brooke is likely to take at the embattled and badly softened-up corporation. Together with the deregulatory effects of the Broadcasting Act 1990 (the bill for which was piloted through by David Mellor in his time at the Home Office) the government inquiry which will take place into the BBC will end what has been a stable tradition of public service broadcasting since the Second World War. On the other hand, issues relating to censorship – regulation of the content of satellite broadcasting, for instance – and exclusive media rights for sport and other cultural events, are fermenting all the time with little sign of a government strategy beyond the ubiquitous 'let the market rule'. Pakistan's victory over England in the cricket World Cup may not have harmed Tory fortunes as much as England's soccer defeat in Mexico in 1970 debilitated Harold Wilson, but Norma Major's satellite dish birthday present to her cricket-mad husband may yet have a long-lasting symbolic importance. BSkyB's anti-ITV coup over television rights to the Premier League (paying £304 million for the privilege) signposts the way that the market is being driven by large (in this case, Rupert Murdoch-owned) corporations prepared to use sport to decimate the competition.

In the related sports field of the soccer industry, there remains the tricky unfinished saga of the Hillsborough stadium disaster report, while its author, Sir Peter Taylor, moves on to grapple with the even more fraught problems of the discredited criminal justice system from his position as Lord Chief Justice. The Football Spectators Bill of 1989 was originally designed to implement the much-ridiculed identity card scheme for soccer spectators in England and Wales. The Act which passed into law is now the vehicle – in the form of the Football Licensing Authority which the statute created – chosen by government to make all Premier and First Division soccer grounds in England and Wales all-seater by 1994. Until recently the rest of the League clubs had to become all-seater by the end of the century, but Mellor, in the weeks before he resigned, signalled the government's intention to be flexible about allowing standing at some smaller soccer clubs. Lord Taylor, as he now is, is said to be unhappy about the somewhat confused debate which has followed the prolonged implementation of his post-Hillsborough proposals, although it is unclear whether his own stance has shifted. One thing is certain: the Taylor Report was never meant to be the juggernaut for driving through all-seater stadiums which cabinet ministers – under pressure to drop the ID card scheme – loudly proclaimed. Safety *not* law and order was in fact the judge's watchword. Loud protests by independent fan organizations such as the Football Supporters' Association (FSA) and pre- and post-election noises from both Labour and Tory Home Office camps have suggested that a new climate of official opinion is emerging. However, the decision of UEFA to hold the European Championships in England in 1996 will ensure that there will not be much modification of the original government concept of the 'end of the terrace'.

The problem in these and other areas of responsibility of the Department of National Heritage is what kind of regulatory regime will be created by a ministry which has already shunned the need for a House of Commons select committee to police the field of policy making in arts, sport and culture. Whether the clues are in the more hawkish pre-legislative position taken on control of the media or in the more conciliatory tone of the jousting on safety at soccer grounds, we shall, for the moment, have to wait and see.

The second question, that of the precise status and shape of the business of pleasure in post-Thatcher Britain, is unfortunately somewhat less open. David Mellor's strident suggestion that the making of money and the making of pleasure – and by implication their regulation, if any – are largely separate was an inauspicious opening gambit for the Department of National Heritage and may prove to be an appropriate epitaph. The production and consumption of 'fun' is as much about industrial production, distribution and exchange as traditional manufacture; in a deindustrializing economy the question is what jobs, skills and products can be created in sectors such as the cultural industries and what regulation is needed. The left in British politics, too, has yet to accept the full implications of many of the regular working and business practices in the cultural industries themselves. Without by any means having been converted to fully fledged Thatcher-style market economics, many of those in pop or video industries see the kind of state (local or national) intervention currently on offer as inappropriate, bureaucratic or just plain unnecessary.

This is not at all to argue for no social intervention in the free market of cultural products. But it is a plea for taking seriously what might be seen as alternative enterprise culture which has grown up – or been further extended – in the Thatcher, and now the Major, years. Witness, as one example, the mushrooming of fan magazines (literally, 'fanzines') around sport and music in particular, aided by desk-top publishing technology and an iconoclastic, entrepreneurial spirit of irreverence. Or take the party craze of the late 1980s and early 1990s (known variously as 'acid house' or 'rave culture') where a libertarian slogan – 'the right to party' – has clouded the more significant individualistic claim which is the right to *organize* parties for profit, a bargaining position overwhelmingly supported by the regular thousands of party-goers often hemmed in by militaristic tactics of police squads equipped for riot.

Unless the new Department of Heritage takes its diverse provinces seriously as *industries*, it is unlikely that Peter Brooke will be able to say 'welcome to the house of fun' as his predecessor's first remarks as Secretary of State suggested; more probably it will turn out to be the 'lion's den' for Heritage, if not the whole Major administration, as the election victory reveals itself to be a poisoned chalice after all.

Meanwhile, Manchester will go on eating itself! The global publicity given to a particular (skewed) vision of events in club and party life since 1988 in the environs of the city has for a time helped to boost the (youth) cultural tourism of Manchester, as an economic region in the depths of a vicious recession which continues to devastate sections of its workforce and its general population. A city cannot live on publicity alone, however. At some stage the reliance on the service economy and the burgeoning cultural industries in the area will have to bear long-term fruit as well as short-term media space. It is to be hoped that, when all the exhibitions and talking shops are over, a strategy for the culture industry can begin to be developed on a regional basis within the new Europe, looking ahead to a time when all the 'hype and type' surrounding drugs, dance and deviance is long forgotten. 'Oh *Madchester*, so much to answer for', as one of the city's most famous sons, Stephen Patrick Morrissey, might have phrased it.

17 Licensed to Thrill

Tourism is a key word of the 1990s, particularly in Manchester youth or pop tourism. Cotton has been replaced by popular culture, and Manchester intends to sell it by the coachload. It is estimated that £230 million is brought into the city each year from tourism alone, and every evening, as the commuters head home, the city centre is invaded by thousands of nocturnal consumers eager for a slice of the postmodern metropolitan experience. Despite *New Musical Express* recently cremating 'Madchester', it is still easier to get a lift on a coach back to Preston, Birmingham or London at 2 a.m. on a Sunday morning than it is to get a taxi to Chorlton-Cum-Hardy.

Leisure is big business, but has Manchester got what it takes to pull in the punters and prise open their wallets? The 'Whitworth Street Corridor' has a mighty pull, but what do the consuming classes do when they leave the Cornerhouse, the Palace Theatre or the Green Room at 11 p.m. or the Hacienda or Venue at 2 a.m.? They go home and, more importantly, they stop spending money. Manchester City Council is more than aware of this and is pushing for the relaxation of licensing in the city, adopting a more European approach (while Europe is copying British practices – clubs in Rimini have been forced to close at 2 a.m. by central government).

Pat Karney, head of the Arts and Leisure Committee (or Chair of Fun, as the *Manchester Evening News* recently called him), has taken on the task of forging a deregulated licensing strategy for the 1990s. He recognizes the dual benefits of deregulated cultural and leisure industries in the city. Karney argues:

> The top priority for the council in the 1990s is the creation and preservation of jobs in Manchester, and this is one of the sectors where jobs are still growing.

Secondly, Manchester is an entertainments centre and I see nothing wrong in people having a good time, a cheerful time, in what is after all a pretty grotty period.

The problem for Pat Karney and other likeminded colleagues at the City Council is that they are hamstrung by a series of archaic statutes. Many have suffered the frustration of the mad dash for last orders, only to get to the bar at 11.05 p.m. Or the early morning search for the after-hours party or illegal 'rave'. In Glasgow, you can drink until 5 a.m., while in London, Brighton and even Mansfield you can dance through until Sunday lunchtime without fear or favour. So why, in a city which aspires to be a civilized European cultural capital, in a country which has deregulated everything from the money markets to the media, are we prevented from drinking and dancing when we want to?

The legal framework is provided by anachronistic licensing laws, but it is their interpretation by local authorities, local police and magistrates which causes added problems. Phil Bell, owner of PJ Bell's on Oldham Street, is in no doubt who is to blame at a local level. Bell says: 'Who can expect licensing magistrates who live in Wilmslow and Altrincham, and who go to bed at 11 p.m., to appreciate what goes on in a city like Manchester?' Further:

> Magistrates don't understand that there are people who want to live a different lifestyle, who want to go out at 11 p.m. and drink in civilized surroundings till the early hours. People have limited resources and energies. They won't go on 24-hour binges, but will reschedule their leisure time. The magistrates can't, or won't, see that; can't see that what we need is flexibility or commonsense.

Licensing is the key to the regulation of the night-time economy, and it is the licensing magistrates who, acting on advice from the police and the council, grant, renew or withhold entertainment or liquor licences. The legal framework has evolved over two centuries, but is consolidated in four main statutes.

According to Lesley Gayle at the City Council:

> The standard entertainment licence is issued under the Local Government (Miscellaneous Provisions) Act 1982. Some local authorities take it as part of their duty to include restrictions on permitted hours, but they can, if they wish, issue a 24-hour, seven days a week entertainments licence (as recently granted for Turnmill's, the Trade club in Islington) and leave the enforcement of the Sunday Observance Act to the police or private prosecution.

The Sunday Observance Act 1780 is in fact a classic pre-modern law. It provides that any place used for entertainment 'upon any part of the Lord's day called Sunday, and to which persons shall be admitted by the payment of money . . . shall be deemed a disorderly house or place'. Unfortunately, it is this atavistic statute which enabled James Anderton ('God's cop', as the Happy Mondays sang) to enforce his own brand of 'moral authoritarianism' and which is still cited by city-centre police today.

Powers to permit and regulate entertainment on Sundays were consolidated in the Sunday Entertainments Act 1932, which sanctions musical entertainment, but not dancing, during licensed hours. By allowing special hours certificates, the Licensing Act 1964 provides for extensions until 2 a.m. (3 a.m. in London), and contemplates that 'dancing and other entertainments as well as music may so continue'. It is under this regulation that people are privileged and able to drink and dance until 2 a.m.

Drink and dance are not mutually exclusive partners, however. Since the 1960s club-goers have been able to maintain those dilated pupils with constructive use of various amphetamine-based substances. By the late 1980s, house music and 'rave culture' had introduced a new drug, ecstasy, and a new 'threat to public order', causing escalating moral panic. British youth, who by the mid-1980s had been dubbed the 'docile generation' by cultural commentators, were once again seen to be revolting into style. Ecstasy had the added advantage of 'enabling white men to dance', and dance all night long. Illegal parties were an inevitable side-effect of the drug, since there was nowhere legal to go after 2 a.m. (except for motorway services!) The legal all-nighters which have since been sanctioned, particularly in London, have reduced the demand for illegal parties.

The Licensing Act 1988 (in force in Greater Manchester in 1990) removed restrictions on afternoon drinking (without the country grinding to an excess halt), but also gave magistrates the option to revoke a licence for a multiplicity of reasons, at any one of the seven hearings throughout the year. By the 1990s, media hype and Manchester's continuing gangland strife enabled local police to enforce the closure of several clubs, including the Hacienda and the now-defunct Konspiracy. The media blitz also spawned a police crackdown on illegal warehouse parties and 'raves', their powers enhanced by the Entertainments (Increased Penalties) Act 1990. The regulation of fun was in the ascendancy.

However, a new decade has surprisingly seen an outbreak of realism emerge. There is a post-Anderton, post-Thatcher agenda of dialogue and co-operation between the regulatory authorities. Karney and others in Manchester had arranged to meet the then Heritage Secretary, David Mellor, to discuss licensing and tourism in the city. Unfortunately, the day they were due to meet, the 'Minister of Fun' decided to rid himself of his ministerial status. Pat Karney is still frustrated by the 'medieval mumbo-jumbo' which informs our licensing, but speaks optimistically about the constructive environment created by Chief Constable David Wilmot and the realistic, practical and co-operative approach being adopted by other metropolitan councils.

Indeed, progress has been made over the recent months and there are plans for an after-hours 'dry' Sunday dance club before Christmas 1992. Entertainment licences have been extended (to at least 6 a.m.) for the Limit's All-Nighter, Ethos at the State, Storm at the No.1 Club, Final Frontier at the Venue and, of course, Flesh at the Hacienda, but the drinking stops at 2 a.m. and the last bus goes at the same time.

Before the vision of a '24-hour city' can be realized, new attitudes to our city centres may have to be adopted. Spaces could, for example, be opened up for all sections of our community, not just clubbers. Café, restaurant and pub life could be allowed to spill out on to the streets and squares. Licensing could be deregulated, so that the streets are populated throughout the night, thereby becoming safer, more relaxed and more European in the process.

The problem with the Karney approach, however, is that deregulation is also a 'Tory' policy. It is not just that figures close to Major such as Ken Clarke like to spend the wee hours listening to jazz at Ronnie Scott's. The deregulated, regenerated city is a 'modern' (that is 'Majorite') Conservative vision, the culmination of Margaret Thatcher's post-election pledge in 1987 to retake 'those inner cities'. None of this means that the licensing laws, and their enforcement, are not in urgent need of wholesale rethink and reform. It does, though, mean that progressive policy-makers need to be careful about taking the 'deregulated' route as the *only* solution to the problems of regulation of the night-time economy – and promotion of the 24-hour city – in the rest of the 1990s.

18 The Last Generation?

Is the present generation of 'youth' properly called a 'lost generation' as so much post-war youth in different countries have been categorized? Or is it more accurately the 'last generation'? In other words, are its conditions of existence and likely future development such that the apparently endless 'linear' progression of youth cultures in the second half of the twentieth century has come to a more or less permanent halt?

As I have pointed out elsewhere (Redhead, 1990), in the 1980s and 1990s 'youth' has increasingly been a category for 'disciplining' and 'policing'. In 1993 in the United Kingdom, it emerged that the Major government was planning by 1996 to ensure that the young unemployed – those under 25 years of age – would have their state benefits cut by 20 per cent when the new Jobseekers' Allowance replaced unemployment benefit. At the time of the announcement – in fact, in a response to a written parliamentary question from a Labour MP – the government gave unemployment benefit at the same level for all age groups, but gave income support at a lower rate for the under-25s. The proposed change in unemployment benefit was, said the Social Security Minister at the time, to be applied in the same way as income support from 1996, on the grounds that younger people have lower earnings expectations and are less likely to be living independently. Such characteristics may well be applied generally to the 'twentysomethings' or 'Generation X' as a global phenomenon at the end of the twentieth century: first, that the financial expectations of that generation are somewhat less compared with *both* earlier post-war generations *and* older sections of contemporary society; and second, that the means for independence from the family and the state – or other regulatory bodies – will be less available than it was in the recent past.

In addition to the proposal on unemployment benefit, the Major government also indicated that it would eventually remove income support from up to 200,000 young people between 18 and 24 who had been jobless for more than a year. Commenting on criticism of pilot schemes which were to be introduced on this basis in two trial areas, ministers said that they recognized the concern which exists in inner-city areas that once people in the 18–24 age group gets used to being unemployed it is difficult for them to obtain permanent employment. John Monks, the Trades Union Congress (TUC) General Secretary, commented that this was a move towards American-style workfare, rather than the welfare which had been traditional in post-war Britain. He argued: 'The government is feeling its way towards workfare by offering dubious schemes in return for benefit. They will not lead to genuine work opportunities. They are simply another reason for keeping people off the dole queues.' The pilot schemes, Monks noted, showed that government was 'targeting the most vulnerable in society'.

In 1992 – a year of re-election for John Major's Conservative government – youth unemployment in Britain was already said to be 'steeply rising'. Indeed, it had nearly doubled since 1990. A report by the Unemployment Unit and Youthaid Charities in 1992 claimed that one in six people aged between 16 and 24 – totalling 888,700 – were unemployed. Official figures at the time showed much lower rates of youth unemployment because government statistics do not include 16 and 17-years-olds without jobs, since they are deemed to be guaranteed places on the Youth Training Scheme (YTS) and are therefore not considered to be unemployed. Half of the jobless youngsters received no state benefit, noted the report, because of what it saw as tough new government rules. Paul Convery of the Unemployment Unit argued convincingly that the lack of job opportunities was hitting young people in the 1990s with such a ferocity that many of them may remain outside the labour market permanently, and that the youth unemployment situation 'threatens to repeat the experience of the early 1980s when thousands of young adults were consigned to a hopeless dole queue and real misery at the very start of their lives.' In the early 1980s when what was misleadingly labelled 'Thatcherism' was coming into its own as a political and economic creed in the United Kingdom, Margaret Thatcher's ministers proclaimed that 'unemployment is no longer an option for 16–18-year-olds' as schemes like YTS were introduced. For some commentators, such measures made it no longer as easy for the young to defer adulthood.

What 'Generation X' represents is a permanent deferment of adulthood, while a process of youth culture as advertising cliché – 'cultured youth' – also erodes childhood in its penetration of the pre-teen market. In the work of some sociologists in Europe, such as Professor Ken Roberts at Liverpool University, trends in very many different countries – such as England, Germany, Poland and Czechoslovakia – have meant that transitions to adulthood have lengthened as a result of the decline in youth employment and the upward expansion of education. The result, for some social scientists, is the creation of a new 'young adult' stage of the life course.

The manifest consequence of these trends is that involvement in youth cultures has been prolonged. Much of the conclusion from this sort of research both in Europe and the United States of America suggests a depoliticization of electorates, now and in the future, because of this prolongation of the 'infantile' young adult stage of the life cycle. In my view this is an overly pessimistic conclusion. What may, in fact, be occurring is a process of 'permanent youth'. Certainly, youth unemployment is fast becoming a permanent social problem, unlike in the 1970s and 1980s when it was perceived to be likely to be a temporary difficulty, or in the 1950s and 1960s when the expanding (male) labour market created an economic demand for youth employment.

As contemporary cultural studies writers such as Paul Willis and Phil Cohen have pointed out, in the 1980s a 'new vocationalist' education policy changed to become part of 'schooling for the dole'. In the 1970s, Willis himself had shown, in a classic contemporary cultural study (Willis, 1978), that school culture in the post-war period had acted, for many working-class youngsters, as a determining factor in them quickly transferring to working-class jobs in the post-school period. In the 1980s and 1990s, it was more a case of 'learning not to labour'. At the end of the twentieth century, as Ken Roberts has argued:

> Occupational careers can no longer be relied on to last for life any more than marriages. Youth was once a brief transitional phase between known and stable statuses, childhood and adulthood. Maybe childhood and youth have now become preparations for adulthoods in which nothing is for keeps. In the higher occupational strata progressive careers remain the norm, for males at any rate, but following their extended transitions many adults face lifetimes in low status and unstable employment. (Roberts, 1992)

19 Club Cultures

Sarah Thornton's book (Thornton, 1995) is a welcome addition to the sociology and popular cultural study of rave culture, the most misunderstood youth cultural phenomenon of the 1990s. Based on her Ph.D. at the John Logie Baird Centre, Strathclyde University, under the supervision of Professor Simon Frith in the early 1990s, it carefully and clearly makes a contribution to theoretical debates about the possibilities and problems of the application of the work of Pierre Bourdieu in the sociology of culture and the erstwhile 'folk devils and moral panics' theory of Stan Cohen (1987) and Jock Young (1971) in the sociology of youth and the sociology of deviance.

Sarah Thornton's account of 'club cultures' begins with the unquestionable statement that 'dance cultures have long been seen to epitomize mass culture at its worst'. A rock ideology – remember the classic US response of 'Disco sucks!' – has long operated to sustain a high/low distinction *within* popular music, privileging 'rock' over 'pop' and, latterly, 'pop' over 'dance'. Thornton legitimately breaks with this rock ideology and provides a serious empirical and theoretical study of how 'rave' culture developed out of a diverse 'club culture' in the late 1980s. She is attentive to the social and historical context of the long emergence of a DJ culture – replacing, or displacing, the rock star system – from as long ago as the 1950s.

Though she does not concentrate on it until the afterword, Thornton's book provides a useful contrast with the cultural studies tradition of youth subcultural work embodied in Dick Hebdige's classic book, *Subculture* (1979). Hebdige relied on the (British) punk subculture of 1976–7 – and earlier, mainly male youth cults from teddy boys to rastafarians – for the terrain on to which he was to project his innovative meshing of literary and social theory. Further, Hebdige was concerned with spectacular British youth subcultures which had already largely disappeared by the time of the book's initial publication in 1979, but which had, significantly, started to become globalized as icons of youth and pop.

The explanatory force of Hebdige's theory of subcultures was always debatable when applied to pre-1979; after 1979 it no longer worked well. The separation of 'youth' and 'pop' in the 1980s and 1990s eroded the rock ideology (though not rock music) which postwar subcultural theory is predicated upon. The fragmentation of the audience(s) for popular music and its culture in the 1990s makes *Subculture* theory outdated. It does not mean there are no subcultures any longer: these abound in youth culture today, but are frequently grounded in market niches of the contemporary global music industry – techno, bhangra, gangsta rap, ambient, jungle – even when they 'originally' came from the 'streets'.

Sarah Thornton provides an interesting update on Hebdige through application of Bourdieu's theory of 'distinction'. She develops – out of an analysis of taste cultures – the idea of 'subcultural capital' in order to situate the club and rave culture of the late 1980s and early 1990s. She goes on to claim, tantalizingly, that 'one could easily re-interpret the history of post-war youth cultures in terms of subcultural capital'.

Where Sarah Thornton's book is also helpful is in her analysis of the moral panic surrounding 'acid house' and subsequently 'rave' culture. In this area she is able to rediscover and update another classic sociology of youth text, Jock Young's *The Drugtakers* (1971). The media development of subcultures is as important as it has always been, though it is, as Thornton shows, never the whole story. 'Ravers' – along with possibly 'New Age Travellers' – are undoubtedly the most significant 1990s youth 'folk devils', able to rival any of the sociologically celebrated 1960s versions like the mods and rockers.

Sarah Thornton has written an interesting book on a fascinating subject. She was one of the earliest sociological students of a club culture which has complex dimensions and is accelerating as quickly as the 'bpm' (beats per minute) of its diverse musical styles. There will hopefully be many more good studies by later students to follow in its wake. For the time being, check out the following reading list on this exploding (and imploding) culture of the 1990s.

Further Reading on Clubcultures

Atkins, A.D. (1995) *Ecstasy, Sorted and On One*. London: A.D. Atkins.
Blincoe, Nicholas (1995) *Acid Casuals*. London: Serpent's Tail.
Fleming, Jonathan (1995) *What Kind of House Party Is This?* London: MIY Publishing.

Geraghty, Geraldine (1996) *Raise Your Hands*. London: Backstreets.

Hewitt, Paolo (1995) *Heaven's Promise*. London: Heavenly.

Kempster, Gary (ed.) (1996) *History of House*. London: Sanctuary.

Kureishi, Hanif (1995) *The Black Album*. London: Faber and Faber.

McKay, George (1996) *Senseless Acts of Beauty: cultures of resistance since the sixties*. London: Verso.

Pesch, Martin and Markus Weiskbeck (1996) *Techno Style: the album cover art*. London: Collins and Brown.

Rose, Cynthia (1991) *Design After Dark: the story of dancefloor style*. London: Thames and Hudson.

Rushkoff, Douglas (1994) *Cyberia: life in the trenches of hyperspace*. San Francisco: Harper.

Saunders, Nicholas (1995) *Ecstasy and the Dance Culture*. London: Nicholas Saunders.

Savage, Jon (ed.) (1992) *The Hacienda Must Be Built!* London: International Music Publications.

Stone, C.J. (1996) *Fierce Dancing; adventures from the underground*. London: Faber and Faber.

Various authors (1995) *Highflyers: clubravepartyart*. London: Booth-Clibbon.

Various authors (1995) *Localiser 1.0: the techno house book*. Berlin: Die Gestalten Verlag.

20 Oasis: (What's the Story) Manchester's Glory?

Oasis are the 'Beatles for the 90s' according to *LA Weekly*. Who needs the Beatles 'anthology' CDs when they can buy the music of Oasis? Their first album, *Definitely Maybe*, has been acclaimed as one of the best and most popular débuts in pop history. Their second LP, *(What's the Story) Morning Glory?*, has already sold 9 million copies worldwide – 3 million in the UK alone – and gone into the No. 1 position in the top 20 in the USA. In three years, Oasis have risen from a small-time 'indie'-label band from a city in the north-west of England to world pop and youth superstars.

It is the songs and sound of Oasis and the culture and politics of the times which make them icons of the last decade of the twentieth century. A book could now be written which does for Oasis and the 1990s what Ian MacDonald's *Revolution in the Head: the Beatles records and the sixties* best-seller did for the Beatles and the 1960s. Like MacDonald's book, the focus could be on the records (and live gigs) – the particular performed combination of words and music – of the band.

The astonishing rise of Oasis to pop culture stardom in the post-Madchester millennial mood of Britain in the mid-1990s is such that nine books have already been published about them. There are already fan books about Oasis. Paul Moody's *Lost Inside* and Jemma Wheeler's *How Does It Feel?* (both published by UFO Music) paint illustrated pictures of the 'rebel rock' and 'bad boy' images of Oasis constructed through the media, heavy with emphasis on drug use (ecstasy, cocaine) and fashionable laddism. Music journalist Mick Middles penned a quick fact-packed history of the Manchester background to the band in *Oasis: round their way*, and the group's ex-roadie Ian Robertson spilled the beans in his kiss-and-tell *Oasis: what's the story?* There will inevitably be many more.

As with all Oasis products and memorabilia, fans consume the books avidly. Distinctive Oasis logo t-shirts – borrowed with official permission by their beloved Manchester City soccer club – adorn hundreds of thousands of young torsos of both genders. Guitar chord songbooks of Oasis tunes sell out as fast as their concert tickets, as buskers in every underground and underpass rush to play acoustic versions of Noel Gallagher's songs rather than Bob Dylan. 'Live forever', 'Don't look back in anger', 'Some might say': these are the folk songs of the mid-1990s.

Oasis' songs are said to evoke the Beatles. In fact just as the Beatles took American R & B – and much else – of the 1950s and reworked it for a new decade, so Oasis 'sample' various pop influences from the rich tapestry of four decades and add to it their own distinctive contribution, stretching pop's cultural form beyond the limits it had already reached when dance music proclaimed 'rock is dead' in the early 1990s. 'You're going home in a fuckin' ambience' was the witty bastardization of one soccer chant in 1993. Since then Oasis' lads belligerence has restored the original meaning, 'you're going home in a fuckin' ambulance', as Noel Gallagher nearly did when a fan leaped on stage to assault him at a gig in Newcastle.

Strangely, though, Oasis are responsible for translating the ecstatic buzz of dance culture into guitar pop. Fans of balladeer Burt Bacharach, the Gallaghers blatantly invoke the early 1970s Rolling Stones, the glitter rock of Slade and T-Rex, the punk rock of the Clash, various rock and heavy metal outfits starting and finishing with Status Quo and the 'naff pop' of the New Seekers as well as the Fab Four's entire back catalogue. Significantly, Oasis completely erase the dance groove which anchored Madchester bands before them in late 1980s clubculture. They are firmly a post-rave rock (and roll) band, a style which puts them in the 'Britpop' camp with Blur and Pulp.

However, Oasis are much more than part of the latest market trend and stand as a signpost for global pop culture at the end of the millennium, breaking America, among other major pop countries, with numerous tours. From the world's first industrial city comes another rebirth of youth and pop culture, as yet relatively unheralded. From the concrete jungle that produced the Hollies, 10cc, Barclay James Harvest, the Buzzcocks, Joy Division, New Order, the Smiths, the Happy Mondays, the Stone Roses, Take That and so many others, the story can be told of a post-war 'pop city' (or 'Bop City' as one of its hundreds of fanzines once had it) whose economy has changed in just forty years from traditional mass manufacture to a reliance on banking, services and popular culture, including sport and the arts, by the end of the millennium.

Manchester made a bid in the early–mid-1990s – judged third alongside Sydney and Beijing in September 1993 – to host the Olympics in the year 2000 and will be the venue for the Commonwealth Games in 2002. The bid symbolizes the social and cultural changes which have occurred, mirroring the attempts of many other world cities to carve out a new role for post-modern culture's urban lifestyle and post-industrial cultural identity in the twenty-first century.

Manchester was the city named by 40 per cent of New Yorkers in an opinion poll in the early 1990s when asked which European city they would most like to visit. Today Manchester is the focus for all kinds of city 'imaging' from Jeff Noon's post-urban sci-fi novels *Vurt* and *Pollen* to the publicity brochures of its burgeoning higher education industry. The city of Manchester has a global reputation as a soccer capital, the label of 'Madchester' became synonymous with youth and pop culture in the late 1980s and early 1990s, and because of international media coverage (such as the front cover and feature article for *Newsweek*) a huge international audience for cultural products from Manchester, mainly among those under 30, male and female, is now guaranteed. This history also covers the pop cultural explosion, the drug gang wars which the tabloids labelled 'gunchester', the making of a once marginalized gay culture into an urbane 'gaychester', the social effects of free-market government policies on the inner city and migration to the suburbs, and the City Council's initiatives to bridge the public/private divide in everything from job creation to the regulation of the night-time economy.

The emerging 'pop city' which is briefly described here is linked to the emergence of Oasis, rooted in Irish immigration and satellite council estates as well as in the new regenerated city-centre flat-dwelling community, as a huge international pop phenomenon of the mid-1990s. Even New Labour's Tony Blair came in for Oasis' 1996 Brit Awards approval – Noel Gallagher has occasionally met the Labour Party leader, who himself used to play in a 1970s rock band – as one of a very few people (apart from Oasis themselves!) who could help carve out a future for youth in the late 1990s and beyond. The question now is how long New Labour and Oasis can last as popular culture and politics career towards the millennium.

Notes

Introduction

1 See further Redhead (1990, 1995).
2 'Cult Studs' is Michael Berube's abbreviated description of Cultural Studies in his discussion of its North American impact in 'Pop goes the academy', first published in the *Village Voice Literary Supplement* in 1992, and reprinted in Berube (1994). I have added the 'Pop'. For an archaeology and genealogy of 'pop', see Kureishi and Savage (1995). For a 'Popular Cultural Studies' reader, see Redhead *et al.* (1997).
3 Redhead (1993) has been used by the British Library to develop the American Library of Congress classification system to create a new subject category, 'rave culture'.
4 The dance culture descriptions continue to proliferate at breakneck speed; witness the following selected list: house, deep house, electro, garage, techno, ambient, gangsta rap, trip-hop, gabber, hardcore, handbag house, euro pop, trance, jungle, tribal. An idea of the variety can be found on good collections such as Ministry of Sound, *Sessions Volume 2*, mixed by Paul Oakenfold (MOS Recordings); Kevin Saunderson/KMS, *The Party of the Year: a compilation album* (KMS); The Aphex Twin, *Selected Ambient Works Volume 2* (Warp); Various Artists, *Classic Electro Mastercuts Vol. 1* (Mastercuts); and Various Artists, *The House Sound of Chicago* (ffrr). Also play the Pet Shop Boys, *Disco* and *Paninaro 95*, Parts 1 and 2 (Parlophone) for an insight into how hi-NRG gay disco music from the USA and continental Europe was given its own British slant. Further, the Pet Shop Boys, *Disco 2* (Parlophone) is also interesting for its remixing, and the Pet Shop Boys, *Alternative* (Parlophone) – a collection of B-sides and assorted other tracks – forms, as Jon Savage points out in the sleevenotes, 'a potted history of club music over the last ten years, both gay and straight: from New York Electro to Euro to House to Acid to spooky Techno'. For a state-of-the-art remix dance record, play New Order, *The Rest Of* (London), a double album which also, uniquely, includes a whole LP of remixes of one classic track, 'Blue Monday'. 'Hard Times' is the name of a club first started in Yorkshire, England and its subsequent record label. Two dance albums celebrate the club: *Todd Terry Live at Hard Times* (Hard Times) and *Hard Times: the album*, mixed by Roger Sanchez (Hard

Times in conjunction with Narcotic Records). For post-Madchester 'Manchester' dance music, play *From Manchester With Love.net* (Love.net).

Chapter 2

1 Patrick Bishop and David Black, for instance, wrote an article entitled 'Thatcher task force on soccer' in the *Sunday Times* on 17 March 1985.
2 *Eastham* v. *Newcastle United FC* 1964 Ch. 413.
3 See, especially, Hopcraft (1968).
4 In his capacity as sports writer for the *Daily Mail*.
5 In his capacity as sports writer for the *Observer*.
6 My thanks to Andy Ward for allowing me to eavesdrop on his father's fascinating reminiscences.
7 Robert Armstrong's article 'Referees reject insurer's hand' in the *Guardian* on 5 March 1981 noted that an insurance company's scheme to help referees prosecute anyone who attacked them on the field of play (player or spectator) or while travelling to or from a game had been criticized because it 'could start a flood of legal cases which do not warrant going to court'.
8 This has actually occurred in Scotland. Davey Cooper of Rangers was charged by the Procurator Fiscal with reckless conduct after an incident in a cup match against Falkirk in which the winger was alleged to have thrown a coin or similar object which struck a 14-year-old boy in the crowd.
9 *The Report of the Inquiry Into Crowd Safety at Sports Grounds* (Cmnd 4952, HMSO 1972).
10 *Guide to Safety at Sports Grounds (Football)* (HMSO, 1976).
11 'Football – our most popular sport', *New Society*, 23 October 1980.
12 See Eric Dunning, John Williams and Pat Murphy, *All Sit Down* (2 vols), report presented to the Football Trust in 1984, which monitored the 'decline and fall' of Coventry City's experiment.
13 Richard Kinsey and Derek Sayer's article, 'A crime to carry a bottle', *New Statesman*, 29 February 1980, articulated fears of what the Scottish law would do for civil liberties.
14 Letters to the *Guardian* on 18 March 1985 called for soccer fixtures to be licensed, echoing an earlier call from *Police*, the magazine of the Police Federation, in September 1983 after the 1983–4 season had opened with 'trouble' at a Brighton versus Chelsea fixture. On that occasion the response from the Association of Chief Police Officers (ACPO) was to reject the call for public order legislation to be used. The ACPO response in 1985 is seen in the figure of the chairman of its special group to monitor the movements of soccer fans throughout the country, much as the National Reporting Centre observed miners' movements during the coal strike of 1984–5. Greater Manchester's chief constable, James Anderton, chaired a conference of chief constables in April 1985 which decided to create a 'data bank' of 'troublemakers': see James Lewis, 'Police to set up data bank on football hooligans', *Guardian*, 26 April 1985.
15 See David Hearst, 'Safety check for Chelsea "cattle fence"', *Guardian* 22 April 1985, and Michael King, 'Chelsea retreat over electric fence', *Standard*, 25 April 1985.
16 *Cawley* v. *Frost* (1977) 64 CAR 20.
17 *Bristol City Football Club* v. *Milkins* (1978), reported in the *Daily Telegraph*, 31 January, page 3.

Chapter 4

1 As they report in 'Tracking down the 6.57 Crew', *Police*, vol. XVII, no. 8, April 1985, p. 42.

Chapter 6

1 Letters page, *New Socialist*, no. 45.

Chapter 8

1 See 'Younger than yesterday', *Melody Maker*, 28 June 1986 'Ladybirds and start-rite kids', *Melody Maker*, 27 September 1986; 'What's missing?', *Monitor*, no. 3.
2 See 'Against health and efficiency', *Monitor*, no. 5; and also Paul Oldfield, 'Beyond freedom and leisure', *Monitor*, no. 2.
3 See Bruce Dessau, 'Shamble city', *City Limits*, no. 237, 17–24 April 1986.
4 For instance, 1950s anoraks and other accoutrements of the distant past obtained from second-hand clothes shops. See Simon Reynolds in *Melody Maker*, 27 September 1986, and the interview with members of Talulah Gosh in the same issue.
5 For an introduction, see Jane Wilkes, 'Morrissey, Sweeties, The Ramones and Shambling . . . ', *Record Mirror*, 4 October 1986. For an account of their stablemates at 53rd and 3rd, Talulah Gosh, see Simon Reynolds in *Melody Maker*, 13 November 1986, particularly for its stress on the incompetence/competence dimension to 'shambling' pop bands like these. Reynolds argues that the music's 'edge' is gained by a striving for musical competence.
6 See *i-D* special 'pop issue', no. 46, 1987; 'Childlike innocence and assumed naivety permeate the Cutie scene – their clothes are asexual, their haircuts are fringes, their colours are pastel. Cuties like Penguin modern classics, sweets, ginger beer, vegetables and anoraks. Heroes include Christopher Robin . . . Buzzcocks and The Undertones.'
7 Mick Middles (1985) notes Morrissey's endless love affair with 1960s girl singers like Sandie Shaw (with whom the Smiths worked and recorded), the prime exponent of the vocal style these groups self-consciously adopt. As Middles says: 'Morrissey obviously saw young Sandie as a lead figure to herald a new age of feminism.'
8 The recording was made by Pete Lawrence, boss of the small, independent label Cooking Vinyl, which has been responsible for recent albums by leading figures in the 'new folk' or 'post-punk folk', the Oyster Band and the Mekons.
9 Gregson, who has had a role as producer of artists like the Oyster Band, is also contracted with Cooking Vinyl. His album with Christine Collister, *Home and Away*, released on Cooking Vinyl, was originally recorded at the duo's live gigs and was available only as a tape sold by them at the end of the night's performance at a folk club.
10 Greil Marcus, 'Speaker to speaker' column, *Artforum*, March 1987.

Chapter 15

1 One possible grid is the following:

Europeans	*versus*	*Latins*
Teamwork		Individualism
Consistency		Inspiration
Level-headedness		Passion

Commitment	Temperament
Rationality	Genius/madness
Results	Performance
Diligence	Drama
Professionalism	Instinct
Honesty	Deceit
Discipline	Flair
Defence	Attack
Workmanship	Showmanship
Masculine	Feminine
Civilized	Savage

References

Anderson, Digby (ed.) (1996) *Gentility Recalled: mere manners and the making of social order*. London: Social Affairs Unit.

Berube, Michael (1994) *Public Access*. London: Verso.

Cohen, Stan (1987) *Folk Devils and Moral Panics: the creation of the mods and rockers*. Oxford: Blackwell.

Dunphy, Eamon (1987) *Only A Game?* London: Viking.

Hebdige, Dick (1979) *Subculture: the meaning of style*. London: Methuen.

Hewison, Robert (1986) *Too Much: art and society in the sixties, 1960–1975*. London: Methuen.

Hill, Dave (1989) *Out of his Skin: the John Barnes phenomenon*. London: Faber and Faber.

Hopcraft, Arthur (1968) *The Football Man*. Harmondsworth: Penguin.

James, C.L.R. (1996) *Beyond a Boundary*. London: Serpent's Tail.

Kureishi, Hanif and Jon Savage (eds) (1995) *The Faber Book of Pop*. London: Faber and Faber.

Marquand, David and Anthony Seldon (eds) (1996) *The Ideas that Shaped Post-War Britain*. London: Fontana.

Middles, Mick (1985) *The Smiths*. London: Omnibus.

Redhead, Steve (1990) *The End-of-the-Century Party: youth and pop towards 2000* Manchester: Manchester University Press.

Redhead, Steve (ed.) (1993) *Rave Off: politics and deviance in contemporary youth culture*. Aldershot: Avebury.

Redhead, Steve (1995) *Unpopular Cultures: the birth of law and popular culture*. Manchester: Manchester University Press.

Redhead, Steve (ed.) with Derek Wynne and Justin O'Connor (1997) *The Clubcultures Reader: readings in popular cultural studies*. Oxford: Blackwell.

Rimmer, Dave (1985) *Like Punk Never Happened*. London: Faber and Faber.

Roberts, Ken (1992) 'Young adults in Europe', Department of Sociology, University of Liverpool.

Shelton, Robert (1986) *No Direction Home*, London: New English Library.

Thornton, Sarah (1995) *Club Cultures*. Cambridge: Polity Press.

Turner, Steve (1976) *Conversations with Eric Clapton*. London: Abacus.

Whannel, Garry (1979) 'Football, crowd behaviour and the press', *Media, Culture and Society*, vol. 1 no. 2.

Willis, Paul (1978) *Learning to Labour: how working class kids get working class jobs*. Farnborough: Saxon House.

Young, Jock (1971) *The Drugtakers*. Harmondsworth: Penguin.

Index